Helena Gomm

Inside Out

Teacher's
Book

MACMILLAN

Macmillan Education
Between Towns Road, Oxford OX4 3PP, UK
A division of Macmillan Publishers Limited
Companies and representatives throughout the world

ISBN 10: 0-333-75764-5
ISBN 13: 978-0-333-75764-2 (International Edition)
ISBN 10: 0-333-96762-3
ISBN 13: 978-0-333-96762-1 (Level IV Pack)
ISBN 10: 0-333-96740-2
ISBN 13: 978-0-333-96740-9 (Level IV Book)

Project management by Desmond O'Sullivan, ELT Publishing Services.
Designed by Ann Samuel.
Illustrated by Martina Farrow and Martin Chatterton p10. Cartoon on
p10 reproduced by kind permission of *Private Eye*.
Cover design by Andrew Oliver.

Printed and bound in Great Britain by Martins the Printers Ltd,
Berwick upon Tweed.

2010 2009 2008 2007 2006
10 9 8

Introduction

At the heart of 'Inside Out' is the belief that the most effective conditions for language learning come about when students engage in activities on a personal level rather than 'going through the motions'. Engagement can be triggered by anything from understanding and smiling at a cartoon to talking at length to a partner about your most treasured possession.

Upper intermediate students

Upper intermediate students are well on their way to becoming competent communicators. They usually have enough language at their disposal which, together with a few tried and tested communicative strategies, enable them to function more than adequately in most situations. They accept that they may still need some remedial work to deal with a few persistent elementary errors but are keen to tackle more complex structures, expand their mental lexicon and develop more of a 'feel' for the language.

- Although they've covered all of the basic grammar thoroughly, occasional 'silly mistakes' will reveal gaps in their depth of understanding of certain structures. A more analytical approach may help iron out these residual problems whilst at the same time encourage them to experiment with more complex language and so maintain a sense of progress and forward momentum.

- They typically have an active lexicon of somewhere between 2,000 and 3,500 words and can recognise many more, particularly if their native language shares the same roots as English. However, a lot of these words and expressions are only half known: they may be unaware of some important collocations as well as the range, connotation and register of the items. Time spent learning more about 'half-known' words is likely to be more useful in the long run than the more natural inclination to race ahead and learn lots of 'brand new' words.

- Although there may still be a few instances where they fail to understand a listening or reading text (an obscure accent or unfamiliar writing genre), they are usually able to get the gist and pick out specific information when required. What they often miss out on – particularly with spoken English – are the hidden layers of meaning where things such as register, accent and unfamiliar cultural references come into play. Understandably, this can be very frustrating and undermine confidence.

Because they can get by in most situations, and because they are more interested in expanding the quantity rather than quality of their language knowledge – more 'new' words rather than more about 'old' words – there is a danger that their 'half-learnt' language will 'fossilise': i.e. that their language deficiencies will become permanent features of their competence.

The challenge this poses to the teacher is to create a situation in the classroom where students consolidate and expand on what they already know, become more fluent in how to use it in both written and spoken forms, and improve their comprehension skills – in particular, their ability to 'notice' more complex aspects of language that may previously have passed them by. *Inside Out* aims to help you do this as easily and efficiently as possible.

Teaching strategies

All the strategies employed in *Inside Out* aim to promote learning by focusing on personal engagement, both intellectual and emotional.

Accessible topics and texts

Each unit is built around a set of two or three related topics. These have been selected to be meaningful to virtually all students: they are subjects about which most people have something to say.

Grammar awareness / grammar practice

The course covers the main grammar areas you would expect in an upper intermediate course book, but in a way appropriate to the needs of upper intermediate students.

At upper intermediate level, there is little point in teaching conditionals in the same way as at lower levels, ie as if the students had never seen them before. Upper intermediate students already know a lot about conditionals – and this applies to most of the structures that are generally taught at this level. But students still want, expect and need grammar to fill gaps in their knowledge and deepen their understanding.

To provide appropriate grammar study, *Inside Out* includes 'Close up' sections. These follow a three stage approach: language analysis; practice; personalisation.

1 The language analysis stage promotes 'noticing' of language features and usage. The language to be 'noticed' almost always comes out of a larger listening or reading text where it occurs naturally in a wider context. We do not believe that self-contained, pre-fabricated example sentences are a good starting point for analysis. At this point students are encouraged to articulate and organise what they know, and incorporate new information.

This stage will work both as individual study or as pair/groupwork. In general, we recommend pair/groupwork as this provides a forum for students to exchange and test out ideas before presenting them in the more intimidating arena of the whole class.

Unlike other books which use the 'guided discovery' approach to grammar, we have generally avoided gap fills and multiple choice questions. Research showed us that most students are unenthusiastic about using these techniques to study grammar. This may be because they associate them with testing rather than learning. Instead, we provide questions and discussion points.

2   In the practice activities students manipulate or select structures, testing their theories. As they do this, they also become more comfortable with the grammar point.

The sentences in this section are designed to be realistic rather than relying on invented scenarios about imaginary people. Many can be applied to the student's own lives, and this facilitates the next stage.

3   The personalisation stage is not a conventional free practice, where students, for example, take part in a role play which 'requires' the target structure. As Michael Lewis has pointed out, very few situations in real life actually require a particular structure. Furthermore, when they are faced with a challenging situation without time to prepare, many students will, naturally, decide to rely on what they know, rather than what they studied half an hour ago. For these reasons, personalisation is based on actual examples of the target structure. Students apply these examples to their own lives, opinions and feelings. Very often the sentences or questions from the practice stage are recycled for the personalisation. For example:

- Replace the names in the sentences in 1 to make the sentences true for you.
- Work with a partner. Ask the questions in 2. Give true answers.
- Work with a partner. Which of the habits in 1 would most annoy you? Put them in order of most to least annoying.

All the Close up sections are supported by Language reference boxes, which give accurate, clear explanations backed up with examples. These appear in the unit, right where they're needed, rather than being tucked away at the back of the book.

Personalised speaking tasks

Inside Out is filled with speaking tasks. Their main purpose is to develop fluency. While they are not intended principally as grammar practice, they are linked to the topics, lexis and grammar in the unit so as to include opportunities for students to turn input into output.

The tasks do not require complicated classroom configurations. They are easy to set up and enjoyable to use. Most of them encourage the students to talk about things that actually matter to them, rather than playing roles or exchanging invented information. Personalised, authentic tasks challenge and engage students, and this encourages linguistic 'risk taking': Can I use this word here? Is this how this structure works? Research into second language acquisition suggests that when students take risks they are experimenting, testing theories about how the language works. This is an essential part of language learning.

Anecdotes

There are also extended speaking tasks, where students tackle a longer piece of discourse. We've called these 'anecdotes'. They are based on personal issues, for instance, memories, stories, people you know. When you learn a musical instrument, you can't spend all your time playing scales and exercises: you also need to learn whole pieces in order to see how music is organised. Anecdotes give students a chance to get to grips with how discourse is organised.

The anecdotes are set up though evocative questions. Students read or listen to a planned series of questions and choose what specifically they will talk about; shyer students can avoid matters they feel are too personal. As they prepare for the anecdote, students also think about the language they will need. This student preparation is a key stage and should not be rushed. Research, by Peter Skehan among others, has shown that learners who plan for tasks attempt more ambitious and complex language, hesitate less and make fewer basic errors.

The simplest way to prepare students for an anecdote is to ask them to read the list of questions in the book and decide which they want to talk about. This could be done during class time or as homework preparation for the following lesson. The questions have check boxes so that students can tick the ones they are interested in. Ask them to think about the language they will need. Encourage them to use dictionaries and make notes – but not to write out what they will actually say. Finally, put them into pairs to exchange anecdotes.

A variation is to ask the students to read the questions in the book while, at the same time, listening to you read them aloud. Then ask them to prepare in detail for the task, as above.

Alternatively, ask the students to close their books – and then to close their eyes. Ask them to listen to the questions as you read them aloud and think about what they evoke. Some classes will find this a more involving process. It also allows you to adapt the questions to your class: adding new ones or missing out ones you think inappropriate. After the reading, give them enough time to finalise their preparation before starting the speaking task.

Repeating anecdotes

Consider going back to anecdotes and repeating them in later classes. Let the students know that you are going to do this. This will reassure them that you are doing it on purpose, but more importantly, it will mean that they will be more motivated to dedicate some time and thought to preparation. When you repeat the task, mix the class so that each student works with a new partner, ie one who has not previously heard the anecdote.

Another approach outlined by Michael Lewis et al. in *Teaching Collocations* (page 91) is to reduce the time allowed to deliver the anecdote each time it is repeated: in the first instance the student has five minutes; for the second telling they have four minutes; and the third three minutes.

Repeating complex tasks reflects real interactions. We all have our set pieces: jokes, stories. And we tend to refine and improve them as we retell them. Many students will appreciate the opportunity to do the same thing in their second language, and research has shown that given this opportunity they become more adventurous and at the same time more precise in the language they use.

You can also use the anecdotes to test oral proficiency and thereby add a speaking component to accompany the tests in the Teacher's Book.

Realistic reading

In theory, no matter how difficult a text may be, the task that accompanies it can be designed to be within the competence of the student, ie 'grade the task not the text'. But conversations with students and teachers have convinced us that this is an insight of only limited value. However easy the task, students are quickly disillusioned by an incomprehensible text.

At the other extreme, many of the texts that have appeared in ELT coursebooks in the past have obviously been written merely in order to include examples of a given grammatical structure. Texts like this are often boring to read and unconvincing as discourse.

The solution adopted in *Inside Out* has been to base all reading texts on authentic modern sources, including magazines, novels, newspapers, websites and personal communications. Where necessary, the source texts have been edited and graded so as to make them challenging without being impossible. The texts have been selected not only for their language content but also for their interest and their appropriacy to the students who will use this course.

Varied listening work

The listenings include texts specially written for language learning, improvisations in the studio and authentic recordings. There are dialogues, conversations, monologues and real pop songs by the original artists. There is a variety of English accents – British, American, Irish, Australian, Scots, North Country – and some examples of non-native speakers. The tasks are designed to develop real life listening skills.

Contemporary lexis in context

Selecting vocabulary to teach becomes more difficult at higher levels. It is relatively easy to predict the needs of beginners: 'hello', 'please', 'thank you'. As learners progress to higher levels, their vocabulary needs come to depend more and more on their individual situations: jobs, courses of study, exams, personal interests, etc.

In *Inside Out* vocabulary is selected to be generally useful and appropriate to the typical student, who is likely to be 17–35 years old and relatively well educated. It is always presented in context and is related to the themes and topics in the unit.

Lexis is first of all highlighted in exercises which draw attention to it, then recycled in back up exercises. The Workbook provides further recycling, as do the photocopiable tests in the Teacher's Book. The exercises encourage students to deal with lexis as part of a system, rather than as a list of discrete words through tasks focusing on collocation, connotation and social register.

Motivating writing practice

The coursebook contains seven structured writing tasks which offer the students opportunities to get to grips with a variety of formats: narrative, discursive, formal and informal letters, CVs and web pages.

This is backed up by a self-contained writing course which runs through the Workbook.

Components

Each level of *Inside Out* includes a Student's Book, a Teacher's Book, a Workbook, Class Cassettes and CDs, a Workbook Cassette and CD, and a photocopiable Resource Pack. The course also includes a Video and a Video Teacher's Book.

Student's Book

The Student's Book covers about 90 hours of classroom teaching. It is made up of 12 main units (1–6 and 8–13) and two review units (7 and 14). The units do not follow a rigid template: the flow of each one comes from the texts, tasks and language points in it.

The book includes all the tapescripts, plus a list of verb structures, information on different types of phrasal verbs, nouns, a glossary of grammatical terminology, a guide to the phonemic alphabet, and a list of irregular verbs.

Class Cassettes (2) and CDs (2)

These have all the listening materials from the Student's Book.

Workbook

The Workbook provides revision of all the main points in the Student's Book, plus extra listening practice, pronunciation work and a complete self-contained writing course.

Workbook Cassette and CD

This contains listening practice and pronunciation work, plus recordings of some of the reading texts.

Teacher's Book

In this book you'll find step-by-step notes and answers for every exercise. These include closed-book activities to warm the class up before beginning a new set of work. The tapescripts are included in the body of the notes for easy reference.

For every one of the main units there is a one-page photocopiable test, for use as soon as you finish the unit or a couple of weeks later. There are longer mid-course and end-of-course tests which go with the two review units (7 and 14).

At the beginning of the book there is a Zero unit. This consists of two parts.

The first part is a quiz about the Student's Book to help familiarise students with it: how language is described, the kinds of activities they will do, how the list of contents works, what they can find at the back of the book.

The second part is a Student profile. It aims to discover something about each student's language learning history and reasons for studying English, for example, for an exam, for academic studies, for work reasons, out of personal interest, etc. Students can fill the form out individually or by interviewing each other in pairs. The Student profile is similar to needs analysis, which has been used in business English for many years. But it is not only business students who have reasons for learning. General English students also have needs and wants. Knowing about them will help you to plan lessons, to use the coursebook more appropriately and to get to know your students better.

Resource Pack

The Resource Pack contains thirty-seven photocopiable worksheets designed to supplement or extend the Student's Book. The worksheets are based on the themes and grammar points in the book and are linked to the book unit by unit. They were written for this project by eleven different ELT teachers. They are very varied, but one thing they have in common is that they provide practical, useful classroom practice. There are full teaching notes for every worksheet.

Video

The video contains one sequence for each unit of the Student's Book. Each sequence links to exercises and pages in the Student's Book, either using tapescripts to create a visual version of listening exercises, or taking a topic and developing it more fully.

Video Teacher's Book

The Video Teacher's Book provides photocopiable worksheets for the video sequences, as well as full keys and tapescripts.

Over to you

If you have any comments about *Inside Out* you will find a feedback form on our website at www.insideout.net, where you can also register to receive extra teaching materials free every week by e-mail.

Zero unit answers

(Page numbers refer to the Student's Book.)

1 a) Twelve (pp 2, 3).   b) They are review units (pp 2, 3).

2 a) can (p 144)   b) yes (p 143)   c) book (p 151)

3 a) Attraction (unit 9, p 87)   b) Ritual (unit 5, p 43)
c) Home (unit 13, p 120)   d) Genius (unit 10, p 97)
e) Money (unit 3, pp 24, 25)   f) Images (unit 1, p 11)

4 Reporting verbs (p 72).

5 Functional language for sympathy, advice and recommendations (pp 34, 35, 36).

6 a) Money (unit 3, p 28);   b) Digital (unit 6, p 61)
c) Home (unit 13, p 122)

7 Lara Croft (p 56).

8 Small Country (p 69)

9 The clockwork radio (p 94).

10 Diego Rivera (p 91).

0 Zero unit

Book quiz

Look through your book and find the answers to these questions.

1. a) How many units are there in the book?

    _____

    b) Why are units 7 and 14 different?

    _____

2. a) What is the first verb beginning with 'c' in the table of irregular verbs?

    _____

    b) Which word illustrates the sound /j/ in the table of phonetic symbols?

    _____

    c) What is the last word of tapescript 35?

    _____

3. Look at the list of contents. In which unit can you:

    a) sing along to *Never Ever* by All Saints?

    _____

    b) read an extract written by Nick Hornby?

    _____

    c) learn vocabulary to describe houses?

    _____

    d) play Trivia pursuit?

    _____

    e) learn about the gold rush?

    _____

    f) listen to four men talk about their self-image?

    _____

4. What grammar structure is dealt with in the Language reference section in Escape?

    _____

5. What can you study in the first two Close up sections of Body?

    _____

6. Look at the list of contents. Decide which units you think these pictures are in and then check in the unit.

a) _____ b) _____

c) _____

7. Who is the star of *Tomb Raider*?

    _____

8. Complete the title of the Bill Bryson book: *Notes From A …*

    _____

9. What is Trevor Baylis famous for inventing?

    _____

10. Who was Frida Kahlo married to?

    _____

Student profile

- **Name**

_____

- **Have you studied English in the past?**

No ☐ Yes ☐ → When and where? _____

- **Have you got any English language qualifications?**

No ☐ Yes ☐ → What are they and when did you take them? _____

_____

- **Do you use English outside the class?**

No ☐ Yes ☐ → When do you use English and where? _____

_____

- **Are you studying English, or in English, outside this class?**

No ☐ Yes ☐ → Please give details _____

_____

- **Do you speak any other languages?**

No ☐ Yes ☐ → Which ones? _____

_____

- **Why are you studying English?**

I need it for work.

No ☐ Yes ☐ → What do you do? _____

_____

I need it to study.

No ☐ Yes ☐ → What are you studying? _____

_____

Where? _____

I'm going to take an examination.

No ☐ Yes ☐ → What examination are you going to take? _____

_____

When? _____

For personal interest.

No ☐ Yes ☐ → What do you like doing in your free time? _____

_____

Photocopiable

1 Images *Overview*

The topic of this unit is image, and this word is interpreted in several ways from important images of the twentieth century to self-image. The main grammatical focus is on verb structure and questions: tag questions and indirect questions.

The unit begins by considering important images from the twentieth century. Students look at photographs and listen to people saying how the events depicted in them affected their lives. They then discuss five years which they see as significant in their own lives or in the history of their country.

Students then move on to looking at the different images of herself that the singer Madonna has created in recent years. They read an article and match sections of it to photographs. They then talk about their own favourite famous people.

Next, students listen to four ordinary people talking about self-image and how this is reflected by their clothes.

The unit ends with a board game which involves asking and answering questions on a variety of personal issues.

Section	Aims	What the students are doing
Introduction page 4–5	*Conversation skills*: fluency work	Talking about photographs of important events in the twentieth century.
	Listening skills: listening for gist	Listening and matching speakers to photographs.
	Grammar: verb structures	Completing texts with appropriate verb structures.
Close up pages 5–8	*Grammar*: verb structures; auxiliary verbs; *so* & *neither*; question tags & short answers; intonation	Studying verb structures; auxiliary verbs, *so* and *neither*. Practising question tags and short answers. Practising sounding interested.
Image queen pages 9–10	*Reading skills*: scanning	Scanning an article to find the correct order of photographs.
	Lexis: collocations	
	Conversation skills: fluency work	Anecdote: talking about your favourite living famous person.
You are what you wear page 11	*Listening skills*: listening for detail	Listening to ordinary people talking about their clothes and their self-image.
	Conversation skills: fluency work	Asking and answering questions about clothes and self-image.
Close up page 12	*Grammar*: indirect questions	Identifying the difference between direct and indirect questions. Practising indirect questions in an information gap activity about David and Victoria Beckham.
Getting to know you – inside out! page 13	*Conversation skills*: fluency work	Playing a board game involving asking and answering questions on a variety of personal issues.

Images *Teacher's notes*

Closed books. Whole class. Tell the class that at the end of the twentieth century an English radio programme had a competition inviting listeners to choose one word that summed up the century for them. Amongst the entries were: *television, communication, materialism* and *war*. Invite the students to discuss in groups and decide what word they would choose.

Then ask them to discuss some of the images of the twentieth century which they find most memorable. These might be newspaper or television pictures, images from advertising or from film. You might like to start them off by choosing your own memorable image and describing it. Again, allow the students to discuss in groups.

1 Books open. Pairwork. Students look at the photographs and make notes under the headings.

Encourage pairs to join other pairs to discuss their findings. When getting feedback, do not discuss the dates of the photographs as these will be tested in the next exercise.

> The four photos show the following:
>
> a   The Berlin Wall coming down (1989). This marked the end of the partitioning of the city in the 1960s following the division of the country into East and West Germany after the Second World War. Reunification of the country followed shortly afterwards.
>
> b   The first man on the moon (1969). Neil Armstrong became the first human being to step onto the surface of the moon. He did so with the famous words, 'This is one small step for a man, one giant leap for mankind.'
>
> c   Nelson Mandela leaving jail on Robben Island with his wife, Winnie (1990). Mandela was jailed by the government of South Africa for his part in the anti-apartheid ANC movement and spent twenty-seven years in prison. Shortly afterwards the apartheid system collapsed, and Mandela became the first black president of a united South Africa.
>
> d   The Sex Pistols (1977). A famous punk band, the Sex Pistols were renowned for their anarchic attitude to authority and the crudity of their song lyrics.

2 Students work individually to match the years and the photos. They can then check their answers on page 136.

> a)   The fall of the Berlin Wall (1989)
>
> b)   The first man on the moon (1969)

> c)   The freeing of Nelson Mandela (1990)
>
> d)   The Sex Pistols (1977)

3   **01 SB p 145**

Ask students to write the names Alex, Beth, Chris and Debra on a piece of paper. Play the recording. As they listen, students note down the letter of the appropriate picture next to the names of the speakers.

> Alex: b   Beth: d   Chris: c   Debra: a

01

Alex

It was the highlight of my whole life because, when I was a kid I always used to think – I hope I live long enough to see a man on the moon. So when it happened – I don't know how old my son was, but I said to him, 'Sit down and watch all of this – this is one of the most momentous things that will ever happen in your life.'

Beth

What annoys me is that people think punk was just a fashion. For me, it was much more than that – it was a way of life. I mean, how long do you think it took to do that make-up and hair? It used to take about four hours a day just getting dressed!

Chris

I'll never forget the day he came out of prison, partly because it was on my birthday, the 11th February, but mainly because it was such a happy event. What I found most amazing about that day was that he'd spent twenty-seven years in prison, and yet he looked as if he had just stepped out for a walk with his wife, as if it was something he'd been doing every day of his life. What an incredible man – and in spite of everything, he doesn't appear to carry any anger or bitterness.

Debra

I was only a kid and I was watching television, when a newsflash came on and I saw these crowds of people climbing on this wall. I had no idea what was going on and I actually thought something terrible had happened. Then I realised people were laughing and celebrating. I'd never heard of the Berlin Wall before that night.

4 Students try to complete the extracts before listening to the recording again to check their answers.

The students' answers may be correct, even if they do not

match the tapescript exactly. If there are differences, discuss why the speakers have used the structures they have.

> **Alex**
> 1 used to think
> 2 live
> 3 happened
> 4 will ever happen
>
> **Beth**
> 1 annoys
> 2 took
> 3 used to take
>
> **Chris**
> 1 'd spent
> 2 had just stepped
> 3 'd been doing
>
> **Debra**
> 1 was watching
> 2 came on
> 3 thought
> 4 had happened
> 5 'd never heard

5 Students work individually at first to write down their five years. They then compare and discuss with a partner.

Optional activity

Find out what the most popular year for the class is. Students mingle, telling each other their years. If one student has the same year as another, they should say why they chose that year. At the end of the mingle, there should be one year that features most. Find out if it's for the same reason in any cases.

Close up (p 5)

Verb structures

1 Allow students to compare answers with a partner before checking with the whole class.

> a) I've known
> b) I had
> c) I was talking
> d) I like
> e) I've been learning
> f) I've been
> g) I'd already met
> h) I used to have

2 Pairwork. Give students a few minutes to work individually on their sentences before they compare them with a partner. Students should look at each other's sentences and ask questions to elicit more information.

Auxiliary verbs (p 6)

1 Students fill the gaps in the questions. They then match the questions and the answers. Check answers with the class.

> a) Have (8)
> b) Does (4)
> c) Are (2)
> d) Were (7)
> e) Do (5)
> f) Had (3)
> g) Did (6)
> h) Has (1)

2 Pairwork. Students take turns to ask questions from 1 and to give true answers. Encourage them to report back to the class any interesting information that they find out.

So & neither (p 6)

1 02 SB p 145

Go through the instructions with the class to make sure students understand that they are listening for things the two people have in common. They should also try to decide why the conversation stops.

Elicit answers from the class, encourage the students to use the expressions *both*, *so* and *neither*. If they have trouble with this, refer them to the Language reference section on page 8.

> They're both American.
> Neither of them is on vacation.
> They're both working in London for a few months.
> Neither of them likes the weather.
> They've both been in London for a few weeks.
> They're both from Santa Barbara, California.
> They both went to Rosefield High.
> Neither of them were very good students.
> They both graduated in 1989.
> They both remember Mrs Rivers, the math teacher.
> The conversation stops because the man says something uncomplimentary about Mrs Rivers – the woman's mother.

> **02**
> (W = Woman; M = Man)
> W: *Excuse me, is it okay if I sit here?*
> M: *Sure, go ahead.*
> W: *Thanks. Sorry, but you're American, right?*
> M: *Right.*
> W: *Oh, me too. Are you on vacation?*
> M: *No, I'm working here for a few months.*

W: *You're kidding – so am I. What do you do?*

M: *I work for the American Central Bank. Pretty boring, huh?*

W: *Oh, no. I mean, a job's a job. ... But you like London, right?*

M: *Er, to be honest, I can't stand it – especially the weather.*

W: *Oh yeah, the weather's terrible. But I love London.*

M: *How long have you been here?*

W: *Oh, not long – a few weeks. How about you?*

M: *The same. What are you doing here?*

W: *I'm an artist, and I was asked to bring over some of my work to a small gallery just near here. I've just had my first exhibition there.*

M: *Wow – that is impressive.*

W: *Thanks – so where are you from?*

M: *I'm from California – Santa Barbara.*

W: *You're kidding – so am I! Don't tell me you went to Rosefield High.*

M: *Yeah, I did – but I wasn't a very good student.*

W: *Me neither. What year did you graduate?*

M: *Um, 1989.*

W: *Oh, that's weird, me too. Do you remember Mrs Rivers?*

M: *Oh, the math teacher? Sure. She was horrible!*

W: *She's my mom.*

M: *Oh.*

2 Elicit an example sentence from the class using the sentence frame. Then give students five minutes to make as many true sentences as they can about the man the woman.

The man is American, and so is the woman.

The man isn't on vacation, and neither is the woman.

The man doesn't like the weather, and neither does the woman.

The man is working in London for a few months, and so is the woman.

The man has been in London for a few weeks, and so has the woman.

The man went to Rosefield High, and so did the woman.

The man wasn't a very good student, and neither was the woman.

The man graduated in 1989, and so did the woman.

The man remembers Mrs Rivers, the math teacher, and so does the woman.

3 Play the recording again for students to listen to and check their answers.

4 Focus attention on the Language toolbox in the margin. Encourage students in groups of three to make up three-line conversations using these expressions, for example:

A: I've got blue eyes.
B: So have I.
C: I haven't.

A: I don't like carrots.
B: Neither do I.
C: I do.

Pairwork. Students decide who they are going to work with, but initially each student works alone. They use the sentence beginnings to write sentences they believe are true both for themselves and the partner they are going to work with.

5 Pairwork. Students play *Bingo!* using the sentences they have written in 4. Go through the instructions with the class before they play in pairs. Students have to promise to give honest answers to the more subjective questions.

Question tags & short answers (p 7)

1 Students replace the underlined parts with expressions from the box. Check answers with the class. If students have problems with question tags, refer them to the Language reference section on page 8.

a) aren't you; Yes, I am; so am I

b) don't you

c) Neither was I

d) so did I

e) Yes, I do

2 🔲 **03 SB p 145**

Give students a few minutes to complete the questions. Then play the recording for them to listen to and check their answers.

a) haven't they

b) do they

c) will you

d) aren't I

e) is it

f) shall we

🔲 **03**

a) *Everybody's arrived, haven't they?*

b) *Nobody likes her, do they?*

c) *Just leave me alone, will you?*

d) *I'm late again, aren't I?*

e) *That's not really true, is it?*

f) *Let's have a drink, shall we?*

3   Pairwork. Students work together to make up a short conversation using three of the tag questions in 2. Encourage confident pairs to act out their conversations for the class.

Sounding interested (p 7)

Closed books. Write a simple sentence on the board, such as *There's a large box on the table*. Read it to the class first with intonation suggesting excitement and then with intonation suggesting boredom. Elicit from the class what the difference is and encourage them to practise reading the sentence aloud in different ways.

Alternative activity

Teacher displays, or even better, elicits a short conversation (eight to ten lines) with the lines numbered. The teacher then hums the conversation once or twice. The teacher then hums individual lines, and students call out the number of the line they think they hear. The students do the same thing in pairs. By the time the students actually say the words of the conversation, their intonation should be much improved.

1   ▭ **04 SB p 7**

Before you play the recording, focus attention on the five short conversations. Make sure students understand that they are to tick the interested responses and put a cross against those where the speaker doesn't sound interested.

Play the recording and allow students to compare their answers with a partner before checking with the class.

a)   ✔
b)   ✗
c)   ✔
d)   ✗
e)   ✔

▭ **04**
a)   *'I don't remember my first day at school.'*
      'Don't you? I do.'
b)   *'I've seen all of Madonna's films.'*
      'Have you? I think she's so boring.'
c)   *'Can you remember your first kiss?'*
      'Yes, I can. Can you?'
d)   *'I loved punk music.'*
      'Did you? I really hated it.'
e)   *'I'll never forget the death of Princess Diana.'*
      'Neither will I. It was so sad, wasn't it?'

2   Pairwork. Students practise saying the conversations aloud. Go round checking that all the responses sound interested.

3   Pairwork. Give students a few minutes to complete the sentences individually. They then work with a partner, taking turns to read out a sentence and give a short

response. Again, go round checking that appropriate interested intonation is being used.

Image queen (p 9)

Reading

1   Closed books. Elicit answers to the two questions here before students open their books. Write up any information or words they use to describe Madonna on the board.

2   Students read the article and try to put the letters of the photographs in the order they are mentioned. They should underline the parts of the article which describe the photos. Give help them with some of the more difficult vocabulary if necessary. (*lips like a red gash*: a gash is a long, deep cut in the skin; *stark*: very bare and plain in appearance; *feisty*: tough, independent and spirited; *uncanny*: strange and difficult to explain; *trends*: changes or developments; *outfits*: an outfit is a set of clothes; *glitzy*: exciting and attractive in a showy way.)

h	e	g	c	f	a	i	d	b

3   Students read the article again and answer the questions. Allow them to compare their answers in pairs or small groups before you check with the class.

a)   Madonna is a very feisty, independent woman. A geisha girl is submissive.

b)   Because it's easy to misunderstand Madonna.

c)   It's a carefully thought-out strategy to get the attention that she wants.

d)   She wants to star in the film adaptation of *Memoirs of a Geisha*.

e)   She adopted an uncanny resemblance to Eva Peron.

f)   She picks up an existing look and makes it her own.

g)   Her platinum blond hair, furs and glitzy jewellery she wore for the video of *Material Girl*.

h)   Because she took her role as Breathless Mahoney very seriously.

i)   Five times (the Jean-Paul Gaultier look; the Brigitte Bardot look; the Earth Mother look; the Indian Mystic look; the Geisha Girl look).

j)   *innocent*

Elicit the students' own opinions of Madonna and her music. Ask them to decide which image in the photographs they think suits her best.

Lexis (p 10)

1   Encourage students to try to complete the gaps without looking back at the text. When they have done as much as they can, they can use the text to check their answers.

a) face

b) burning

c) talent

d) adaptation

e) took

f) adopted

2 Pairwork. Students decide if any of the sentences in 1 are true for them and discuss them with a partner.

Anecdote (p 10)

(See the Introduction on page 4 for more ideas on how to set up, monitor and repeat 'anecdotes'.)

Go through the list of questions with the class. Make sure they understand that these questions are just to give them ideas on what to talk about. They aren't meant to work slavishly through them.

Give students plenty of time to choose their famous person and to decide what they are going to say. Give any help with vocabulary and language that they need.

Pairwork. Students take turns to talk about their famous people.

You are what you wear (p 11)

Closed books. Ask students to say what the last item of clothing they bought was. Get them to describe it, to say why they bought it and to say how they feel when they wear it and what they think it says about them. You could start them off by talking about your last clothing purchase.

1 Students look at the photographs. Elicit which one they like best. Have a class discussion on what images they think the men are trying to project and why. Put the numbers 1 to 4 on the board and make notes under each one of what the students say. Keep the notes for comparison when the students have done 2.

2 ▭▭ **05 SB p 145**

Play the recording. Students listen and see how what the speakers say compares with their ideas in 1.

▭▭ **05**

(J = Journalist; C = Charles; R= Rick; A = Alan; M = Matt)

Charles

J: *Excuse me! Hello.*

C: *Hello.*

J: *I work for CHAPS magazine, and we're doing a survey about men's self-image. Um, do you mind if I ask you a couple of questions?*

C: *Oh. No, no, go ahead. What do you want to know?*

J: *Well, um, I'd like to know what your clothes say about you.*

C: *What do my clothes say about me!? Gosh – I suppose they say that I'm meeting a client this afternoon, and that means I've got to make the right impression. So I have to wear a suit.*

J: *And would you say you care about your image?*

C: *Oh yes, I think I do. I like to look smart, even when I'm not working. Even when I wear jeans and a T-shirt, I like them to be clean and neat, and I think this says that I care about myself. It says that I've got good self-esteem.*

Rick

J: *Excuse me.*

R: *Me?*

J: *Yes, hi there! I'm working on a feature for CHAPS magazine about men's personal style. Um, do you mind if I ask you some questions?*

R: *Er, no, I suppose not.*

J: *Could you tell me what image you're trying to achieve?*

R: *Image? I don't really have an image. I wear clothes I feel comfortable in – I suppose you'd call it a casual look.*

J: *Hm, and would you say that you're aware of fashion?*

R: *Er, probably not, no. My style hasn't changed for years.*

Alan

J: *Excuse me, sir. Is it okay if I ask you a couple of questions for an article I'm doing for CHAPS magazine?*

A: *Yes, that's fine. Are you going to take photos?*

J: *Er, yes, if you don't mind. But first I'd like to know whether your appearance affects your life in any way.*

A: *Oh yes, totally. The way I dress is my life really. It hasn't really affected my career so far, but I'm hoping it will. Basically I want to be noticed, and the reason I want to be noticed is that I want to get on television.*

J: *Ah. And could you tell me what the last thing you bought was?*

A: *Oh yes, I adore shopping. Er, that would be the pink shirt I bought yesterday – oh, and the pink and black tie.*

Matt

J: *Hello! I'm doing some research for an article about the way men dress. Er, can I ask you some questions?*

M: *Yeah, no problem.*

J: *Do you mind telling me what you wear to go out in the evening?*

M: *In the evening? What, you mean clubs and that sort of thing?*

J: *Yes, when you go clubbing.*

M: *Well, I dress exactly like this.*

J: *You don't dress up then?*

M: *Well, put it this way – I don't put a suit on. The clubs I go to don't let men in if they're wearing suits.*

J: *Really!? Well, how strange. Um, one more question? I'd just like to know if there's an item of clothing you couldn't live without.*

M: *Trainers. Definitely couldn't live without them. I've got about twenty-five pairs.*

3 Give students a few minutes to construct the questions using the cues. Allow them to compare notes with a partner.

4 Play the recording again for students to listen to and check their answers.

a) I'd like to know *what your clothes say about you.*

b) Would you say *you care about your image?*

c) Could you tell me *what image you are trying to achieve?*

d) Would you say that *you are aware of fashion?*

e) I'd like to know *whether your appearance affects your life.*

f) Could you tell me *what the last thing you bought was?*

g) Do you mind telling me *what you wear to go out in the evening?*

h) I'd just like to know *if there is an item of clothing you couldn't live without.*

5 Groupwork. Students discuss the question in groups, then report back to the class.

6 Pairwork. Students take turns to ask and answer some of the questions in 3.

Close up (p 12)

Indirect questions

1 Do the first one as an example, then give students a few minutes to change the questions. If students have problems with direct and indirect questions, refer them to the Language reference section on page 12. Check answers with the class.

a) What do your clothes say about you?

b) Do you care about your image?

c) What image are you trying to achieve?

d) Are you aware of fashion?

e) Does your appearance affect your life?

f) What was the last thing you bought?

g) What do you wear to go out in the evening?

h) Is there an item of clothing you couldn't live without?

2 Pairwork. Students compare the two sets of questions and discuss the three analytical questions. Check answers with the class.

a) Direct questions: question word + verb + subject.

Indirect questions: question word + subject + verb.

b) No.

c) In *Yes/No* questions.

3 Encourage students to work individually at first to correct the questions. They can then compare answers with other students. Check answers with the class.

a) Do you know how much **she weighs**?

b) I'd like to know how old **she was** when she joined *The Spice Girls*.

c) I want to know if **she has** got any pets.

d) Have you any idea what **she thinks** of Madonna?

e) Could you tell me who **her favourite designers are**?

f) Do you know why **he shaved** his head?

g) I'd like to know if **he has** got any tattoos.

h) Could you tell me which football club **he plays** for?

i) Have you any idea which position **he plays** in?

j) I want to know what **his star sign is.**

4 Students look at the photo of the Beckhams. Brainstorm some information about them with the class.

Pairwork. Students turn to their respective pages and read the information given. They then take turns to ask the questions.

5 Pairwork. Students take turns to ask their partner three more questions about Victoria and David Beckham.

Getting to know you – inside out! (p 13)

You will need sufficient dice and counters for each group. Students follow the instructions and play the game.

Test

At the end of each unit there is a photocopiable test. Use it at the end of the unit, or a couple of lessons later. Allow about 30 minutes for it. It scores 40 points: to get a percentage, multiply the student's score by 2.5. You may not wish to use a grading system, but if you do the following is a possibility.

35–40 = A (excellent)   25–34 = B (good)   20–24 = C (pass)

To make the test more complete, add an oral and/or a written component. For example, ask the students to talk in pairs about their family or write an e-mail describing their home town to a new penfriend.

Scoring: one point per correct answer unless otherwise indicated.

1
1. 've known
2. was waiting
3. used to be
4. 's studying
5. doesn't agree
6. 've been training
7. wasn't made
8. 'd already left
9. met

2
1. are
2. don't
3. has
4. Did
5. haven't
6. was
7. Do
8. 's
9. were

3
1. Neither can I.
2. Neither have I.
3. So would I.
4. So was I.
5. So did I.
6. Neither am I.
7. Neither will I.
8. So would I.

4
1. have they?
2. shall we?
3. did you?
4. mustn't she?
5. were they?
6. won't he?
7. is it?
8. will it?

5
1. Would you mind telling me how you know about this?
2. Would you mind telling me when you found out?
3. Would you mind telling me where you saw them?
4. Would you mind telling me who you told?
5. Would you mind telling me what you are going to do about it?
6. Would you mind telling me if you would accept a cash settlement?

1 Images Test

Name: **Total:** _____ /40

1 Verb structures *9 points*

Put the verbs into an appropriate tense.

1   We _____ (know) each other for years.

2   He _____ (wait) for a bus when he saw them.

3   I _____ (be) very shy but now I'm more confident.

4   She _____ (study) three languages at the moment.

5   My sister _____ (not agree) with animal testing.

6   They _____ (train) for this since last summer.

7   This computer _____ (not make) in Japan.

8   She _____ (already leave) when we arrived.

9   I _____ (meet) Mark yesterday morning.

2 Auxiliary verbs *9 points*

Add appropriate forms of *be*, *do* or *have*.

1   What _____ you doing this evening?

2   I _____ like this music. Can we change the CD?

3   How long _____ he lived in this flat?

4   _____ you study English at your last school?

5   We _____ seen her at all since this morning.

6   She _____ walking home when she met him.

7   _____ you ever go to that café in Bridge Street?

8   He _____ been to South Africa several times.

9   They _____ stopped for speeding last night.

3 *So & neither* *8 points*

Agree with these statements.

1   I can't swim yet. _____

2   I've never been there. _____

3   I'd love a coffee. _____

4   I was really bored. _____

5   I used to like it. _____

6   I'm not doing that again. _____

7   I'll never go there again. _____

8   I'd keep quiet if I were her. _____

4 Question tags *8 points*

Complete the questions.

1   Nobody's arrived yet, _____ ?

2   Let's go home, _____ ?

3   You didn't know her, _____ ?

4   She must have left, _____ ?

5   They weren't late again, _____ ?

6   He'll do it again, _____ ?

7   That's not right, _____ ?

8   Nothing will stop her, _____ ?

5 Indirect questions *6 points*

Rewrite using *Would you mind telling me ...?*

1   How do you know about this?

_____ ?

2   When did you find out?

_____ ?

3   Where did you see them?

_____ ?

4   Who have you told?

_____ ?

5   What are you going to do about it?

_____ ?

6   Would you accept a cash settlement?

_____ ?

2 Family Overview

The topic of this unit is family relationships. The main grammatical focus is on verb patterns and adjective patterns.

Students start by considering the relationships between parents and teenagers and read an article about teenagers who are embarrassed by their parents.

Students discuss what qualities parents look for in their children's boyfriends/girlfriends and then listen to interviews with a girl's parents and her boyfriend who are about to meet for the first time. They go on to practise using the appropriate spoken register in different social situations.

The work on register in spoken language is extended by examining the difference between formal and informal written language, and students write informal letters to a penfriend, describing their families.

Section	Aims	What the students are doing
Introduction page 14–15	*Conversation skills*: fluency work	Talking about relationships between teenagers and parents.
	Reading skills: reading for gist	Reading an article about teenagers with embarrassing parents.
Close up pages 16–18	*Grammar*: verb patterns: verb + *to*-infinitive; *make & let*; verb + *-ing* form; verb + preposition structures; single vowel sounds	Studying different verbs patterns using *to*-infinitive, *-ing* form and prepositions. Writing phonetic symbols for single vowel sounds.
Meeting the parents pages 19–20	*Conversation skills*: fluency work	Discussing what qualities parents consider important in their children's partners.
	Listening skills: listening for detail	Listening to a girl's parents and her boyfriend talking about meeting each other for the first time.
	Lexis: phrasal verbs	Replacing verbs in a text with phrasal verbs from an interview.
	Conversation skills: fluency work	Anecdote: talking about a couple you know very well.
Close up page 21	*Grammar*: adjective structures: adjective + *to*-infinitive and adjective + preposition	Practising using different adjective patterns in questions and answers.
Do come in page 22	*Conversation skills*: register	Choosing appropriate language in different social situations.
Correspondence page 23	*Writing skills*: formal and informal letters	Identifying the difference between formal and informal written language. Writing an informal letter to a penfriend.

2 *Family* *Teacher's notes*

Closed books. Whole class. Write the names of your immediate family on the board. Tell the class these people are your family and invite the class to ask you questions about them. For example:

Who's Annie?

She's my sister.

Is she older than you or younger than you?

She's older than me.

And who's Bill?

He's my brother-in-law. He's married to Annie.

Students can then write the names of their own families on pieces of paper and ask and answer questions in groups.

Reading (p 14)

1 Focus attention on the title of the text on page 15: *Problem parents*. Elicit reasons why parents can be a problem to their children and why children can be a problem to their parents.

Pairwork. Students look at the photographs on page 14 and speculate on the answers to the questions. They then take turns to tell each other about their experiences with their own parents or guardians.

2 Give students plenty of time to read the article. Check comprehension by asking students to say in their own words why each of the teenagers regards their parent as a problem. Then elicit opinions on which of the teenagers they would least like to be. You might like to have a class vote on the question.

3 Encourage students to work individually to match the people with the sentences. Allow them to compare answers with other students before checking with the class.

1	Kayleigh
2	Gina
3	Alex

4 Go through the example with the class. Students then work individually to rewrite the sentences. Check answers with the class.

> a) Kayleigh wanted to the ground to open up and swallow her.
> b) Kayleigh tries to run away as fast as she can.
> c) Kayleigh's mum makes her cuddle her in front of the whole crowd.
> d) Gina's mum loves being in the limelight.

> e) Gina can't stand being the centre of attention.
> f) Gina's mum manages to stay in shape.
> g) Alex dreaded his friends finding out what his father did.
> h) Alex's dad made him join in the act.
> i) Alex never wanted his father to have a boring job.

5 Pairwork. Make sure students have understood that the expression *she wanted the ground to open up and swallow her* means that she was extremely embarrassed. Students take turns to tell their partners about a time when they felt very embarrassed. Be sensitive to the fact that some students may find this rather a difficult subject to talk about. Encourage anyone who is willing to tell their story to the class to do so, but don't force anyone who is unwilling.

Close up (p 16)

Verb + *to*-infinitive

1 Read the sentences with the class and go through the verb patterns with them. Elicit which highlighted verbs correspond to which verb pattern. If students have trouble with these verb patterns, refer them to the Language reference section on page 18.

> Pattern A: sentences a) and c)
> Pattern B: sentence b)

2 Pairwork. Encourage students to do this by fitting the verbs in the box into the pattern sentences and reading them aloud to see if they sound right. Check answers with the class and elicit that *expected, wanted* and *would like* can be used with both patterns.

> Pattern A: *aimed, expected, hoped, wanted, would like, decided*
> Pattern B: *encouraged, expected, reminded, wanted, allowed, would like*
> *expected, wanted, would like* can fit into both verb pattern A and verb pattern B.

3 Give students time to copy the diagram into their notebooks. They then put the boxed words into the appropriate places. Check answers with the class.

> Pattern A: *helped, intended, can't afford, attempted, offered, paid, refused, planned, preferred*

Pattern B: *helped, taught, invited, ordered, paid, warned (not), urged*

The following verbs can fit into both verb pattern A and verb pattern B: *helped, paid.*

4 Read the sentences with the class and elicit opinions on how the verb patterns differ.

These verbs (*make* and *let*) take an infinitive without *to.*

5 Pairwork. Students first work individually to match the beginnings and endings of the rules They then discuss their sentences with a partner and decide if they agree with the parents' rules.

Suggested answers
a) We wouldn't let them *hitch-hike by themselves.*
b) We'd expect them *to respect their elders.*
c) We'd make them *keep their rooms tidy.*
d) We wouldn't let them *smoke in the house.*
e) We'd tell them not *to believe everything they hear.*
f) We'd warn them not *to take drugs.*
g) We'd let them *go out late at the weekend.*
h) We'd make them *take their studies seriously.*
i) We'd encourage them *to keep fit.*
j) We'd ask them not *to play their music too loud.*
k) We'd want them *to do well at school.*

Optional activity

Invite students to work in groups to prepare a list of children's rules for parents. These could be general rules or rules aimed at limiting the embarrassment they cause their children.

Verb + -*ing* form (p 17)

Students will find more information about these structures in the Language reference section on page 18. You might like to ask them to read this first before doing the first exercise.

1 Students fill the gaps with the words in the box. Check answers with the class.

a) borrowing
b) studying
c) buying
d) embarrassing
e) ironing
f) having
g) talking

2 Pairwork. Students discuss whether the sentences in 1 are true for them or not.

Verb + preposition structures (p 17)

There is more information on these structures in the Language reference section on page 18. Refer students to this if they need help.

Optional activity

Ask students if they have ever been to another country. If they have, ask why they went abroad. Was it for a holiday, work or study? Find out if the country was as they expected it to be. Did they find it easy to adapt to the differences?

1 **06 SB p 146**

Give students time to read Eva's sentences and decide on the correct order. Allow them to discuss this in pairs or groups if they wish. Then play the recording for them to listen to and check their answers.

1 a   2 e   3 l   4 h   5 c   6 j   7 b   8 i   9 k
10 g   11 f   12 d

📼 **06**

I knew that there were a lot of things I would have to get used to when I decided to go to England and stay with a family. But I was looking forward to having egg and bacon for breakfast and tea at five o'clock. I was also dreaming of the charming English country cottage I would be staying in. I was a bit worried about the reserved British character. I'd heard that they objected to talking about anything personal but insisted on talking about the weather all the time. Nor did they approve of hugging or kissing, apparently. So imagine my surprise when my English family welcomed me with a big hug and then asked me about my family, my work and even my boyfriend. They didn't live in the country cottage I'd dreamt of, and we never had English breakfast or tea at five. But they succeeded in making me feel at home, and I felt as if I belonged to the family for the few weeks I was there.

2 Pairwork. Check that students understand that the expression *things turned out better than expected for Eva* means that Eva didn't think things were going to be very good, but in fact the reality was much better than she thought. Students take turns to tell each other a story about when things turned out better than they expected.

3 Go through the examples with the class. Students then work individually to complete the statements so that they are true for them. They then discuss them with a partner.

Single vowel sounds (p 18)

Your students may or may not be familiar with the international phonetic alphabet. This alphabet is very useful for finding out the pronunciation of new words and it is worth spending some time going through the symbols and example words with students. (See page 143 in the Student's Book.)

1 📼 **07 SB p 18**

You could play the recording and ask students to write down the symbols for the sounds they hear. Alternatively, you could get them to write the symbols before they listen to the recording, predicting what the vowel sounds will be. (Note that the symbols have been numbered *1–12* for easy identification.)

> a) (9) /æ/, (1) /ɪ/
> b) (10) /ʌ/, (8) /ɔː/
> c) (11) /ɑː/
> d) (7) /ɜː/, (5) /e/, (12) /ɒ/
> e) (4) /uː/, (2) /iː/
> f) (3) /ʊ/, (6) /ə/

2 Focus attention on the meaning of the sentences in 1. Ask students to match them with their meanings. You could do the first one with the whole class as an example.

> a 3   b 6   c 5   d 2   e 4   f 1

3 Pairwork. Students discuss which of the sayings they like best.

Meeting the parents (p 19)

Closed books. Find out if students have ever taken a boyfriend or girlfriend home to meet their parents. Ask them how they felt about it beforehand and what happened. Did they ask their parents to behave in particular way to their friend? Did they ask their friend not to mention certain subjects in front of their parents? If students are unwilling to talk about a boyfriend or girlfriend, they could discuss taking any friend home to meet their parents.

Groupwork. Students read the list of points and decide on their answers to the questions. Encourage them to give reasons for their decisions when they report back to the class.

Listening (p 19)

Students look at the photos of Sarah and Andy and Sarah's parents. Elicit what kind of people they think they are and some words they could use to describe them.

1 📼 **08 SB p 146**

Go through the instructions with the class so they are clear about the situation. Read the sentences and make sure students know that as they listen they have to decide whether they are true or false.

Play the recording. You could play it a second time if students find it hard to decide whether some statements are true or false.

> a) True   b) False   c) True   d) False   e) False

📼 **08**

(I = Interviewer; M = Mum; D = Dad)

I: *So you're going to meet Sarah's boyfriend tomorrow?*

M&D: *That's right.*

I: *How do you feel about that?*

M: *Well, we're looking forward to meeting Andy at last – we've heard a lot about him, because Sarah's been going out with him for a while now. Several weeks, I believe.*

I: *Does Sarah usually bring her boyfriends home to meet you?*

D: *Well, it's difficult to know with Sarah really – she changes boyfriends like other people change their socks. We've met some of them.*

M: *Yes, I'd say we've met half a dozen over the years.*

I: *Have you liked most of her boyfriends?*

M: *No, not really. I'm always amazed at how awful they are. She goes for very strange types. There was just one we liked, wasn't there?*

D: *Oh, yes – you mean Jeremy. Lovely chap. We were impressed with him.*

M: *But he didn't last long. As soon as we told her we liked him, she dropped him.*

I: *What sort of person would you like Sarah to go out with?*

M: *Well, I think it's essential for him to come from the same kind of background.*

D: *Yes, and it's very important for him to have some kind of qualifications – you know, some ambition.*

M: *He needs to be a strong character to stand up to Sarah – she'd soon go off somebody who lets her do what she wants all the time.*

D: *Oh, anyway, we're not going to take it too seriously. She's far too young to get married or engaged or anything like that. And the poor chap is unlikely to last very long.*

2 Encourage students to work individually to choose the appropriate verb patterns to complete the sentences. Play the recording for them to check their answers.

> a)   to meeting
> b)   to know
> c)   to come
> d)   to have
> e)   to be
> f)   do
> g)   to last

3 🔲 **09 SB p 146**

Go through the sentences with the class. Play the recording. Students listen and mark the sentences true or false.

a) True   b) True   c) False   d) False   e) False

🔲 **09**

(I = Interviewer; A = Andy)

I: *How do you feel about meeting Sarah's parents?*

A: *A bit nervous. I'm worried about making a bad impression because I'm quite shy. So I find it difficult to get on with people straight away.*

I: *But you're a DJ, aren't you?*

A: *Yeah, but it's easy for me to hide behind my music decks at work. I'm not very good at making conversation, especially with older people.*

I: *What are you most nervous about?*

A: *Well, I gave up studying to become a DJ, and I don't think Sarah's parents will be very impressed with that. Also, I, I dyed my hair last week, and they'll probably be a bit shocked by that.*

I: *How are you going to try and make a good impression?*

A: *Well, I'm going to wear clean clothes – not a suit or anything. I haven't got one. And I'll take her mum some flowers.*

I: *Why are you going to meet Sarah's parents?*

A: *Because Sarah fancies going to London for the day, and she feels like having Sunday lunch at home. And I always do what she wants.*

4 Students work individually to complete the sentences. Then play the recording again for them to check their answers.

a) meeting
b) making
c) to hide
d) making
e) studying
f) to make
g) going; having

Lexis (p 20)

Students work individually to replace the underlined words with verbs from the box. Allow them to compare answers with a partner before checking with the class. Students then discuss the statements in pairs, saying whether or not they are true for them.

a) get on with
b) go off
c) gone out with
d) stand up to
e) gave up
f) go for

Anecdote (p 20)

(See the Introduction on page 4 for more ideas on how to set up, monitor and repeat 'anecdotes'.)

Pairwork. Go through the instructions and the questions with the class. Give students time to decide who they are going to talk about and what they are going to say. They then take turns to tell a partner about their couple. Encourage the listening partner to ask questions to elicit further information at the end.

Close up (p 21)

Adjective structures

1 Students write three sentences, using ideas from the table on a piece of paper. If you like, you can encourage them to use the structures in the first three columns but provide sentence endings of their own. They should not write their names on the paper.

2 Collect the folded pieces of paper and shuffle them. Give a piece to each student. Students then mingle around the room trying to find the student who wrote the sentence on their piece of paper. They do this by asking questions following the question structure outlined in the book. As soon as they have found the correct person, they should sit down.

3 Students work individually to see how much they know about adjective + preposition structures. When they have finished, you can direct them to the Language reference section if they need more information about these structures.

a) at   b) for   c) on   d) of   e) to   f) in   g) with
h) about

4 Pairwork. Students take turns to ask and answer the questions in 3.

Do come in (p 22)

Register

1 Establish that the two conversations are similar in that both involve people arriving at someone else's home. Ask students what the relationships are between the people arriving and the people whose home it is. Ask how well they know each other. (In Conversation 1, the two people are friends – boyfriend and girlfriend. In Conversation 2, Andy is arriving at his girlfriend's parents' house and he hasn't met them before. Sarah is visiting her parents.) Get students to predict which conversation will use more formal language (that between Andy and Sarah's parents).

Students read the conversations and decide which of the alternatives to choose for each gap. Do not check answers at this stage.

2 ▭ **10 SB p 146**

Play the recording for students to listen to and check their answers. Ask several students to predict how long Andy and Sarah will continue going out together and encourage them to give reasons for their predictions.

> Conversation 1
> 1 a 2 b 3 a 4 a 5 a 6 b 7 a 8 b 9 a
> 10 b
> Conversation 2
> 1 b 2 a 3 b 4 b 5 b 6 a 7 b 8 a 9 b
> 10 a

▭ **10**

Conversation 1

(S = Sarah; A = Andy)

S: *Hello!*

A: *Hiya. The door's open!*

S: *Here, I remembered to bring you that CD.*

A: *Oh, cheers – that's great!*

S: *How's it going?*

A: *All right. I'm totally shattered.*

S: *Why? What've you been up to?*

A: *Nothing – it's just that I didn't finish work until five o'clock this morning.*

S: *Oh right. Well, you'd better just chill out this evening. Do you want to watch telly, or shall I go and get a video?*

A: *Whatever.*

S: *Do you know what's on telly tonight?*

A: *Oh, no idea. Rubbish as usual, I should think.*

S: *Oh dear, you're in a bad mood. You're not nervous about meeting my parents, are you?*

A: *No. Why should I be? But I am a bit worried about the long drive. My car's on its last legs.*

S: *Oh well, let's worry about that tomorrow. Come on – make me a nice cup of tea.*

Conversation 2

(M = Mum; D = Dad; S = Sarah; A = Andy)

M: *Hello. Welcome. Do come in.*

S: *Mum, Dad, this is Andy.*

M&D: *Nice to meet you.*

A: *Nice to meet you. These are for you – Sarah says they're your favourites.*

M: *Oh, thank you – that's very kind of you. And how are you, darling?*

S: *I'm absolutely exhausted, actually.*

M: *Oh dear. What's the matter? Have you been working too hard?*

S: *Oh no, nothing like that – it's just a long drive, isn't it?*

M: *Yes, of course. You must sit down and relax, both of you. Would you prefer coffee or tea, Andy?*

A: *I don't mind. Whatever's easiest.*

D: *How many miles is it exactly?*

A: *Oh, I'm afraid I don't know. The journey's taken us five and a half hours, but my car is rather old.*

D: *Oh yes, I always take the A420, followed by the A34, except during the summer when I tend to avoid motorways and go through Winchester on the backroads.*

M: *Well, we're not going to talk about roads all day, are we? Now Andy, what exactly do you do? Sarah tells us you're in the music industry ...*

3   Groupwork. Students discuss the advice they would give and then report back to the class on their conclusions.

4   Pairwork. Give students plenty of time to choose their situations and work out what they are going to say. Encourage confident pairs to perform their conversations for the class.

Correspondence (p 23)

Formal & informal letters

Closed books. Divide the board into two columns with the headings 'Formal' and 'Informal'. Then brainstorm the following questions: Who would you write a formal letter to? Who would you write an informal letter to? Write these questions up on the board and then elicit some of the conventions you would associate with each style (eg an informal letter starts with *Dear* + first name, uses contractions, ends *Love* + first name; an informal letter starts with *Dear* + title and surname / *Sir* / *Madam*, doesn't use contractions, contains more passive structures, ends *Yours faithfully/sincerely*).

1   Pairwork. Students discuss the questions.

2   Students read the letter. Elicit the answer to the question.

> It is an informal letter which contains a lot of formal letter features.

3   Give students time to decide which of the informal expressions can be used to replace the underlined words and expressions in the letter. Check answers with the class, then elicit answers to the final question.

```
1 l   2 q   3 m   4 a   5 f   6 s   7 o   8 i   9 c
10 e  11 n  12 j  13 k  14 t  15 b  16 p
17 r  18 h  19 g  20 d
```

In informal letters you don't usually include the addressee's address. You also don't usually include the writer's full name under the signature.

4 Students work individually to write their letters. This can be done as homework, if you wish. Alternatively, you may wish to ask the students to write their letters in class so that you have the opportunity to go around and help them.

5 Pairwork. Students exchange letters and write replies.

Test

Scoring: one point per correct answer unless otherwise indicated.

1
1　f (or e)
2　c
3　a
4　g (or a)
5　b
6　h
7　d
8　e (or a)

2
1　to go
2　to ski
3　driving
4　talking
5　to leave
6　to work
7　moving
8　to meet
9　to lend
10　to have
11　going

3
1　embarrassing
2　to think
3　tell
4　to have
5　to open
6　broadcasting
7　to accept
8　go
9　having
10　to do

4
1　c
2　a
3　e
4　b
5　d

5 (½ point per correct answer)
1　✓
2　✗
3　✓
4　✓
5　✗
6　✓
7　✗
8　✓
9　✗
10　✗
11　✓
12　✓

Name: _____   **Total:** _____ /40

---

1 Adjective patterns *8 points*

Match the adjectives with the prepositions.

1	hopeless	a)	about
2	famous	b)	on
3	serious	c)	for
4	proud	d)	to
5	dependent	e)	with
6	interested	f)	at
7	allergic	g)	of
8	fed up	h)	in

2 Verb patterns *11 points*

Underline the correct form.

1   I wanted **to go / going** to the play but I couldn't.

2   My brother taught me **to ski / skiing** last year.

3   I don't mind **to drive / driving** you to the airport.

4   You can't avoid **to talk / talking** to them now.

5   He ordered them **to leave / leaving** immediately.

6   She always encouraged me **to work / working** in the film industry.

7   My brother is considering **to move / moving** to Portugal.

8   We've arranged **to meet / meeting** up next Friday.

9   He refused **to lend / lending** me his motorbike.

10   His parents wouldn't allow him **to have / having** a party while they were away.

11   Why do you insist on **to go / going** to these places?

3 Verb patterns *10 points*

Complete the text with the correct verb form.

I was always accusing my parents of (1) _____ (embarrass) me when I was younger. My dad loved (2) _____ (think) that he was trendy. He made me (3) _____ (tell) him what clothes were fashionable and then he'd try (4) _____ (have) knowledgeable chats with my friends about the latest trends. I wanted the ground (5) _____ (open) up! And I really objected to my mum (6) _____ (broadcast) to the world all the stupid things I did, and she refused (7) _____ (accept) that she was making a fool of me in front of my friends. And she wouldn't let me (8) _____ (go) out with new friends until she had met them first. Anyway, I'm looking forward to (9) _____ (have) children of my own one day because I've promised myself not (10) _____ (do) the same to them!

4 Vocabulary – social register *5 points*

Match the formal words with the informal equivalents.

1	moreover	a)	anyway
2	in conclusion	b)	by the way
3	consequently	c)	also
4	incidentally	d)	as for me
5	personally	e)	so

5 Pronunciation – single vowel sounds *6 points*

Are the vowels indicated single vowel sounds? Mark them ✓ or ✗.

1	s<u>i</u>mple ☐		7	h<u>o</u>pe ☐
2	cr<u>o</u>wd ☐		8	b<u>oo</u>k ☐
3	<u>a</u>rm ☐		9	h<u>o</u>me ☐
4	p<u>e</u>n ☐		10	l<u>ou</u>d ☐
5	c<u>a</u>me ☐		11	h<u>u</u>gging ☐
6	w<u>a</u>ter ☐		12	togeth<u>e</u>r ☐

3 Money Overview

The topic of this unit is money. The grammar focus is on metaphor, articles, unreal conditionals and linking words.

Students read about the gold rush in California in 1849 and the story of Sam Brannan, who made a fortune selling equipment to hopeful gold miners.

Metaphors, expressions and sayings connected with money are studied and discussed.

Students use unreal conditionals to say what they would do if they governed their country

Students listen to four people talking about their most treasured possessions. They then talk about this subject in pairs.

Finally, students complete a text about an imaginary day in the life of a very wealthy person using linking words and further details which they make up themselves. They then write an account of what a perfect day for them would be like.

Section	Aims	What the students are doing
Introduction page 24–25	*Reading skills*: scanning for specific information	Scanning a text about the California gold rush to find the links between groups of items.
		Listening to the text and putting a summary in the correct order.
	Lexis: collocations	Using collocations from the text to write sentences about yourself.
	Listening skills: listening for detail	Listening to a story, discussing the significance of pictures and matching beginnings and ends of sentences.
Time is money page 26	*Grammar*: metaphor	Studying metaphors from the previous reading text.
		Practising using money and food metaphors.
Close up pages 27–28	*Grammar*: articles; schwa /ə/	Completing a text with articles and matching examples with rules.
		Practising the pronunciation of schwa /ə/ in unstressed syllables.
Money talks pages 29–30	*Lexis*: financial expressions	Looking at expressions to do with money and talking to a partner about finance.
	Listening & speaking skills: listening for detail; predicting; discussion	Listening to an interview and matching questions and answers.
		Predicting how people will answer questions about money.
		Discussing questions about money.
Close up pages 30–31	*Grammar*: unreal conditionals	Matching clauses to make unreal conditionals.
		Studying the structure of real and unreal conditionals.
		Discussing unreal situations.
Treasured possessions page 32	*Listening skills*: listening for gist	Listening to people talking about their possessions and matching them with notes.
	Conversation skills: fluency work	Reconstructing stories in pairs.
		Anecdote: talking about treasured possessions.
A day in my very wealthy life page 33	*Grammar*: linking words	Using linking words to complete a text.
	Speaking skills: adding detail	Adding details to a story to make it more interesting.
	Writing skills: narrative	Writing the completed story.

3 Money *Teacher's notes*

Optional activity

Write the following sayings about money on the board.

Time is money.
A fool and his money are soon parted.
Money doesn't grow on trees.
Money talks.

Students read the sayings about money and discuss what they mean. Ask them if they have similar sayings about money in their language. If your class is multicultural, encourage people of different nationalities to translate any sayings about money that they have into English and explain what they mean to the class.

> a) Time is a resource – just like money.
>
> b) If you are a fool, you are likely to spend money when you shouldn't.
>
> c) Money isn't free – it has to be earned.
>
> d) If you have a lot of money, you can usually get your own way.

Alternative activity

Ask your students: Why was everyone hurrying to California 150 years ago? Ask them what they know about the gold rush (eg How long did it last? Did everyone get rich? etc.).

Reading (p 24)

1 Go through items a) to c) with the whole class. If you like, get students to predict what the links will be. Accept any ideas, however unlikely, and note them on the board.

Give students plenty of time to read the article – it is quite long – and then elicit the links. Encourage students to make sentences using the given words which explain the links between them.

> a) John Sutter came to California to build his own private empire. When the Forty-Niners came, his dream turned to disillusion.
>
> b) James Marshall was building a sawmill on the American River when he saw a piece of gold half the size and shape of a pea.
>
> c) President James Polk's statement to Congress in December 1848 started the gold rush. Hundreds of thousands of people journeyed to the west to look for gold. They were called the 'Forty-Niners' because they left home in 1849.

2 Go through the words in the box with the class. Have a show of hands on who would use each one to describe either John Sutter or the one of the Forty-Niners. If there is any disagreement, encourage students to give reasons for their choices.

> a) John Sutter: visionary, farmer, businessman, conservative
>
> b) One of the Forty-Niners: risk-taker, opportunist, dreamer, entrepreneur

3 ▭ **11 SB p 24**
Play the recording for students to listen to. Allow them to follow the text in their books if they want to. They then number the lines of the summary in the correct order.

> 1 b   2 c   3 a   4 f   5 d   6 e

Lexis (p 25)

1 Students work individually to make more collocations with the words in the box. When they have finished allow them to compare answers with other students. Check answers with the whole class.

> a) *take* a chance, a risk, advantage of the hotel facilities
>
> b) *made* a fortune, money, a mess of his exams, sense
>
> c) *had* no idea, a think about it, a go at skiing
>
> d) *created* a sensation, an atmosphere, the right conditions

2 Students choose their collocations and write sentences. Go round the class asking students to read some of their sentences to the class.

Alternative activity

Get students to write their sentences on pieces of paper with their names at the top. Collect their papers and shuffle them. As you read the sentences out to the class, students put their hands up and try to guess who wrote them. They score one point if they guess correctly. Keep a tally of the scores and see who gets the most points. If you like, you can introduce a more complicated system of scoring with higher points being awarded to someone who guesses correctly after only one sentence of each group of five is read out.

Listening (p 25)

1 ▶ **12 SB p 146**

Students look at the pictures and captions. Establish that they are going to listen to the story of one of the first people to make a fortune from the gold rush, Sam Brannan. Play the recording.

Pairwork. Students discuss the significance of the pictures.

> During the gold rush, Sam Brannan had the only store between Yerba Buena and the gold fields. He bought up all the picks, shovels and prospecting pans. Then he sold them to the Forty-Niners and made a lot of money. In the end, though, he died of alcoholism.

▶ **12**

During the gold rush, Sam Brannan became one of the most successful businessmen in California. He arrived in California in 1846 with a group of two hundred Mormons who had left New York to escape religious persecution. They had made the journey by sea, and on arrival in San Francisco (then called Yerba Buena) they had tripled the city's tiny population.

When gold was discovered on John Sutter's land in 1848, Sam Brannan owned the only store between San Francisco and the gold fields. Quickly recognising a gap in the market, he bought up all the picks, shovels and pans he could find, and then ran up and down the streets of San Francisco shouting 'Gold, gold on the American River!'

He had no intention of digging for gold! No, he was planning to sell shovels. And having cornered the market, he ended up with a lot more gold than the person who had to dig for it.

This was a man who keenly understood the laws of supply and demand. A metal pan that sold for twenty cents a few days earlier, was now available from Brannan for fifteen dollars. In just nine weeks he made $36,000. He became the first gold rush millionaire within a few years.

In the end, though, Sam Brannan lost his fortune and his health, as did many of those who first benefited from the gold rush. Alcoholism finally led to his downfall, and California's first millionaire died an unnoticed death.

2 Play the recording again. Students match the beginnings and endings of the sentences. Play the recording again and let students check their answers.

> a 2   b 4   c 6   d 3   e 7   f 5   g 1

Time is money (p 26)

Metaphor

1 Students look at the words in the box. Elicit what they all have in common.

> They are all to do with water (specifically the movement of water).

Before students turn to their dictionaries, encourage anyone who knows any of the words to explain the meaning to the class. Make sure that everyone is quite certain of the meanings before moving on to the subsequent exercises.

2 If students are unfamiliar with the word *metaphor*, explain that a metaphor is a way of describing something by comparing it to something else that has similar qualities. This comparison is made without using the words *as* or *like* (when these words are used, we call the expression a simile). The words in the box in 1 all refer literally to the movement of water but can be used metaphorically to describe the movement of other things, for example people.

Students use the words in 1 to complete the gaps. Encourage them to do this without looking back at the text. They can discuss it in pairs or groups if they wish. When they have finished, they can look back at the text to check their answers.

> a) trickle, flood, deluge
>
> b) drifted
>
> c) streamed

3 Go through the words in the box with the class, then students work individually to complete the gaps. Allow them to compare answers with a partner but don't check answers at this stage.

4 ▶ **13 SB p 147**

Play the recording for students to listen to and check their answers.

> 1   spare
> 2   valuable
> 3   worth
> 4   wasting
> 5   profitably
> 6   half-baked
> 7   chewing
> 8   food
> 9   digest
> 10 running out
> 11 spend

📼 13

(M = Martha; D = Dad)

M: *Morning!*

D *You're in a good mood today. Any particular reason?*

M: *Yes, there is actually.*

D: *What – in love again?*

M: *No – I've decided to become a millionaire.*

D: *You've decided to become a millionaire. I see. And how exactly do you propose to do that?*

M: *Well, if you can spare a couple of minutes I'll tell you.*

D: *Martha, you know how valuable my time is ...*

M: *Oh, Dad, I promise you it will be worth your while.*

D: *Okay – but just five minutes or else I'll be late for work..*

M: *Right. I've got this idea for a website ...*

D: *Oh come on, you're wasting your time if you think you can make money out of the Internet. All the best ideas have been used up. You should be using your time more profitably getting a proper job ...*

M: *All right, all right. Look, I promise you it's not some half-baked idea. It's something I've been chewing over for the last few weeks. Please just have a look at these plans, then tell me what you think.*

D: *Hm, hm, yes, interesting. There's certainly food for thought here. Er, how are you going to find the money to do it?*

M: *Ah, well, em, I was rather hoping you might help me. Oh will you?*

D: *Well, I can't tell you until I've had time to digest all this information. But you've certainly got a good idea. It's very original.*

M: *But we're running out of time. If we don't do it very soon, somebody else will.*

D: *Yes, you could be right. Look, I've got to go now, but as soon as I get back from work I'll spend the rest of the evening looking at it. Have you told anybody else your idea?*

M: *No, not yet.*

D: *Well, don't ... I think you've really got something here.*

Optional activity

Ask students to discuss what they think Martha's bright idea is. Have they got any ideas of ways to make money out of the Internet?

5 Pairwork. Students read the statements and discuss whether or not they agree with them. Use their feedback as the basis for a class discussion.

Close up (p 27)

Articles

1 **📼 14 SB p 147**

If students have trouble with articles, refer them to the Language reference section on page 28 for more information. Students complete the text. When they have finished, play the recording for them to check their answers.

> a) 1 –   2 a   3 –   4 an   5 the   6 the   7 The
>   8 a   9 –   10 The   11 the   12 a   13 a   14 a
>   15 –   16 a   17 –   18 the   19 the   20 the
>
> b) 1 a   2 –   3 a   4 the   5 the   6 the   7 the
>   8 the

📼 14

a)

A tourist in Africa was walking by the sea when he saw a man in simple clothes dozing in a fishing boat. It was an idyllic picture, so he decided to take a photograph. The click of the camera woke the man up. The tourist offered him a cigarette.

'The weather is great. There are plenty of fish. Why are you lying around instead of going out and catching more?'

The fisherman replied: 'Because I caught enough this morning.'

'But just imagine.' the tourist said. 'If you went out there three times every day, you'd catch three times as much. After about a year you could buy yourself a motor-boat. After a few more years of hard work, you could have a fleet of boats working for you. And then ...'

'And then?' asked the fisherman.

'And then,' the tourist continued triumphantly, 'you could be calmly sitting on the beach, dozing in the sun and looking at the beautiful ocean.'

b)

There was a young lady from Niger,

Who smiled as she rode on a tiger.

They came back from the ride

With the lady inside

And the smile on the face of the tiger.

2 Pairwork. Students work together to find an example of each rule in the texts. Check answers with the class.

> a) Text a): 1; Text b): 2
>
> b) Text a): 3, 9, 15, 17
>
> c) Text a): 2, 4, 8, 12, 13, 14, 16; Text b): 1, 3
>
> d) Text a): 6, 7, 10, 11, 18; Text b): 4, 5, 6, 8
>
> e) Text a): 5, 19, 20; Text b): 7

3 Pairwork. Students first work individually to write their statements. Pairs take turns to discuss their statements and then report back to the class.

Schwa /ə/ (p 28)

Elicit what the schwa sound is (the unstressed sound at the end of such words as *mother* and *Africa*) and establish that the sound is used for most unstressed vowels in English.

1 **15 SB p 28**

Encourage students to read the sentences aloud and decide which vowels to underline. Play the recording for them to check their answers.

> a) Money makes the world go round.
> b) There's no such thing as a free lunch.
> c) Put your money where your mouth is.
> d) In for a penny, in for a pound.
> e) Watch the pennies, and the pounds take care of themselves.
> f) The love of money is the root of all evil.

2 Ask students what they notice about the listed words.

> Usually these words are unstressed, and they are pronounced using a schwa.

3 Pairwork. Students discuss which of the sayings they like best. Encourage them to give reasons.

Money talks (p 29)

Lexis

Books closed. Ask the students to say what they think the saying *Money talks* means. (You can get whatever you want / persuade people to your point of view / get people's attention if you have money.) Ask them to say whether they think it is true.

1 Ask students to work individually to see how many of these money expressions they know. Allow them to consult a dictionary when they have done as much as they can without one. Check answers with the class.

> a) breadwinner – The main breadwinner is the principal money-earner (in a family).
> b) a rainy day – To save (some money) for a rainy day means to save for a time in the future when you might really need it.
> c) broke – To be broke means to be without any money.
> d) blown it – To blow money on something means to spend it all on something.
> e) splashed out – To splash out on something means to spend extravagantly on something.
> f) a fortune – To be worth a fortune means to be worth a lot of money.

2 Pairwork. Students discuss their experiences of the six situations.

Listening & speaking (p 29)

1 Students work alone or in pairs to match the questions and answers. Don't check answers at this stage.

2 🔲 **16 SB p 147**

Students listen to the interviews with Patti, Eric and Lee and check their answers.

> a 3   b 5   c 6   d 2   e 4   f 1

> 🔲 **16**
>
> (I = Interviewer; P = Patti; E = Eric; L = Lee)
>
> **a)**
>
> I: *It's impossible to have too much money – do you agree with that, Patti?*
>
> P: *Yes. If you have dreams, money makes them possible. Personally, I can't imagine having too much money. I'm always broke. Anyway, if I ever felt I had too much money, I'd give it away to charity.*
>
> **b)**
>
> I: *And Patti, would you prefer fame or fortune?*
>
> P: *Being practical, I'd say fortune, but if I were single with no kids and no responsibilities, I'd go for fame.*
>
> **c)**
>
> I: *Eric, were you given or did you earn pocket money as a child?*
>
> E: *I was given two shillings a week by my father, but on condition that I behaved myself. If I didn't behave well, I didn't receive it. Parents were much stricter in those days.*
>
> **d)**
>
> I: *And Eric, what was the first thing you saved up for and bought yourself?*
>
> E: *Oh, a set of toy soldiers. Not the plastic ones you get nowadays, but little metal ones, beautifully hand-painted. It took me nearly a year to save up for them. If I'd known that they would be valuable antiques today, I would've kept them. They'd probably be worth a fortune now.*
>
> **e)**
>
> I: *Tell me, Lee, if you could buy yourself a skill, talent or change in your appearance, what would it be?*
>
> L: *Well, there are lots of things I'd like to be better at, but if I had to choose one, it would have to be football – I'd like to be a brilliant football player!*

f)

I: *And finally Lee, what can't money buy?*

L: *Happiness. I tend to think that once I have enough money to buy some new clothes or get a better car, then I'll be happy. But it never works out like that.*

3 🔊 **17 SB p 147**

Pairwork. Before students split into pairs, elicit what kind of people Patti, Eric and Lee are and how old the students think they are. (Patti is in her late thirties; Eric is in his seventies; Lee is in his late teens.)

In pairs, students read the two questions and discuss how they think the three people would have answered them. Give them time to make a decision before you play the recording for them to check their answers. Find out if any of the pairs guessed correctly.

> a) Patti: It wouldn't matter to her, but it might to her husband.
>
> Eric: He would feel a failure.
>
> Lee: It wouldn't worry him.
>
> b) Patti: She'd splash out on a family holiday.
>
> Eric: He'd buy a new computer.
>
> Lee: He'd blow it on a new stereo system and some massive speakers.

🔊 **17**

(I = Interviewer; P = Patti; E = Eric; L = Lee)

a)

I: *Does it matter if a wife earns more than her husband? How would you handle it?*

P: *It wouldn't matter to me, but it might matter to my husband. It shouldn't matter, but human nature being what it is, it probably would.*

E: *I would feel like a failure if my wife earned more than I did. It's a man's job to earn a living, and a woman's place is in the home.*

L: *It wouldn't worry me. I know loads of couples where the woman is the main breadwinner, and I think that's fine so long as both people enjoy what they're doing. In fact, it would be really good to have a wife who's earning a fortune. But actually, I'm probably not going to get married.*

b)

I: *If you were given £1,000 to save, spend or invest in just one day, what would you do with it?*

P: *Um, the sensible thing to do would be to save it for a rainy day or pay off my overdraft, but I think I'd rather splash out on a family holiday. We need it.*

E: *Do you know what – I think I'd be tempted to get a new computer, because I spend quite a bit of my time on the Internet, and my computer's getting a bit slow. Yes, a new computer, that's what I'd spend £1,000 on.*

L: *Well, I certainly wouldn't save or invest it – I'd probably blow it on a new stereo system and some massive speakers.*

4 Pair or groupwork. Students ask and answer the questions in 1 and 3 for themselves.

Close up (p 30)

Unreal conditionals

If students need more information about conditionals, refer them to the Language reference section on page 31. You might like to go through this first with the class to remind them of the form and use of conditionals.

1 Students match the *if*-clauses with the main clauses. Check answers with the class.

> a 6   b 3   c 5   d 1   e 4   f 2

2 Pairwork. Students discuss the questions. Check answers with the class.

> a) Two.
> b) b, c, e, f
> c) would
> d) The verb moves one step back into the past.

3 Whole class. Read the sentences aloud and elicit answers to the questions.

> In a), the verb in the *if*-clause is *weren't*. In b), the verb in the *if*-clause is *wasn't*. They are both grammatically correct, and there is no difference in meaning between the two sentences.

4 Groupwork. Students discuss the situations. When they have finished, encourage them to report back to the rest of the class.

5 Pairwork. Students first work individually to complete the sentences (you might want to do one first as an example). Make sure they understand that they have to be true for them. They then take turns to discuss their sentences with a partner.

Optional game: Consequences

Students choose one of the sentence stems in 5 and complete it, writing it at the top of a clean sheet of paper. They then pass their piece of paper to their left. The next student takes the subordinate clause and makes it the main clause and finishes the sentence any way they wish. Students pass their pieces of paper to the left and continue in the same way until each student receives their original piece of paper with a series of consequences from their sentence.

For example:

If I had had famous parents, I would have been rich.
If I had been rich, I would have bought a yacht.
If I had bought a yacht, I would have sailed around the world.
If I had sailed around the world, I would have met lots of interesting people.

Treasured possessions (p 32)

Books closed. Ask students to imagine that their house is on fire. All the people and any animals have got out safely and they now have to leave. They can take two possessions with them. What two things would they save and why? Encourage a brief class discussion.

Listening (p 32)

1 Focus students' attention on the photographs and the things the people are holding. Ask them to say why they think these things are special to these people.

2 ▭ **18 SB p 148**

Give students time to read the notes before you play the recording. Students then listen and match the possessions with the notes. Check answers with the class.

> a 3 b 1 c 4 d 2

▭ **18**

a) Armando

It used to be my father's, and I learnt to write on it. Now it's a museum piece. My father thought I might become a musician. He was Daniel Almoia Robles, a famous Peruvian composer and storyteller who created El Condor Pasa. He gave it to me when he realised that I wasn't going to follow him into music. I value greatly other means of expression, like sound technology and cinematography, but when I write, I don't need anything else. When I lived alone in the Peruvian jungle for ten years, I took it with me, and I think that was the period when I wrote more than at any other time in my life.

b) Katie

My mother gave it to me rather than to one of my two sisters – maybe because she realised I was the least likely to get one of my own. I don't wear it because I'm afraid of losing it. I keep it on my bedside table. I see it when I wake up every morning. It's by far my most treasured possession. When I look at it, I remember my mum, who is living in England.

c) Heather

This is my most valuable possession because it saved my life when I got caught in an avalanche in

Johnson Pass in Alaska's Chugach Mountain Range. *It had been snowing for four days and the temperature rose that morning – perfect avalanche conditions. When the first person in our group of snowboarders leaped off the cornice, the rest of us decided to follow his tracks – no traversing and no hard turns, so as to not disturb the snow. When it was my turn, I made it down the first pitch safely and thought I was out of danger. But the person behind me started before I was at a safe distance and nervously made a hard right turn. I heard a loud crack, and then WHOMPH! The snow hit me really fast in the back of the neck. I pushed my neck-warmer over my face, which kept the snow out of my mouth and nose, allowing me to breathe as the avalanche swept me up. I began frantically swimming and tried to stay aware of which way was up. When the snow finally settled, I had managed to get part of my glove up through the surface. It took the others a few minutes to find me, but I knew they would. Luckily, my neck-warmer allowed me the extra air to wait out those few minutes.*

d) Mike

I know it sounds a bit stupid, but this is the thing I'd least like to lose. It's not because it's worth anything, although it is quite an expensive one because it's got e-mail on it too. But the main thing is that if I lost this, I'd lose the addresses and numbers of practically everybody I know. It contains the details of about three hundred people.

3 Pairwork. Play the recording again. Students then work in pairs to reconstruct the stories using the notes. They can either do this orally or they can write the stories down. When they have finished, encourage confident pairs to tell or read their stories to the class.

> a) Armando's typewriter used to be his father's. His father was a famous composer and storyteller. When Armando lived alone in the Peruvian jungle for ten years he wrote a lot on the typewriter.
>
> b) Katie's mother gave her the wedding ring. Katie doesn't wear it because she doesn't want to lose it. She keeps it on her bedside table. When she looks at it, she remembers her mother, who is living in England.
>
> c) Heather's neck-warmer saved her life when she got caught in an avalanche. She pushed the neck-warmer over her face, which kept the snow out of her mouth and her nose. This allowed her to breathe until she was rescued.
>
> d) Mike's mobile phone is quite an expensive one because it's got e-mail on it. But the main reason Mike doesn't want to lose it is that he'd lose the addresses and numbers of the people he knows. His phone contains the details of about three hundred people.

Anecdote (p 32)

(See the Introduction on page 4 for more ideas on how to set up, monitor and repeat 'anecdotes'.)

Pairwork. Give students time to read the questions and decide what they are going to talk about. They then take turns to talk about their most treasured possessions. Encourage the listening partners to listen actively - to make noises of encouragement and agreement, and to ask questions where appropriate.

A day in my very wealthy life (p 33)

Optional activity

Ask your students to look at the picture of the woman. Ask them to describe her and what type of person they think she is. Ask them to predict how they think she would spend a typical day.

Linkers (p 33)

1 Students work individually to complete the text with the linkers in the box. Make sure they understand that they can use each one only once.

1	when / as soon as
2	Then
3	while
4	After
5	As / Just as
6	until
7	During
8	As soon as / When
9	By the time
10	Just as / As

2 Pairwork. Give students plenty of time to prepare for this. You might also like to do the first part (describing the view) yourself as an example. Students take turns to read their texts, adding details of their own at the places marked with letters. Stronger students might like to try doing this without writing the details down first. Weaker students may prefer to write them down, or at least make notes.

3 This writing exercise can be set for homework, if you wish. Make sure students understand that they must use all the linkers from the box in 1 in their compositions.

Test

Scoring: one point per correct answer unless otherwise indicated.

1
1. have
2. make
3. have
4. take
5. create

2
1. A
2. –
3. a
4. a
5. the
6. –
7. a
8. The
9. the
10. an
11. –
12. the

3 (2 points per correct answer)
1. 'd had
2. won
3. 'd have gone
4. 'd be
5. wouldn't mind

4
1. A fool and his money are soon parted.
2. The love of money is the root of all evil.
3. Money doesn't grow on trees.

5
1. winner
2. rainy
3. splashed
4. broke

6
1. as soon as
2. Then
3. while
4. During
5. until
6. by that time

3 Money Test

Name: _____   **Total:** _____ /40

1 Verb + noun collocations *5 points*

Complete the noun and noun phrases with *take, make, have* or *create*.

1   _____ a go at something

2   _____ sense

3   _____ a go at hang gliding

4   _____ advantage of someone

5   _____ the right conditions

2 Definite & indefinite articles *2 points*

Complete the newspaper article with *a/an, the* or – .

(1) _____ man was yesterday ordered to pay (2) _____ £126,000 for sending (3) _____ former employer libellous e-mails under (4) _____ false name. In (5) _____ first British case of its kind, (6) _____ experts traced three messages to (7) _____ laptop computer used by James Richards. (8) _____ e-mails, sent under (9) _____ name 'Kerrie Jones', falsely accused building company boss David Kerley of (10) _____ affair. Richards, of (11) _____ London, denied sending (12) _____ messages.

3 Unreal conditionals *10 points*

Put the verbs into an appropriate form.

1   If I _____ (have) enough money, I would have lent you some.

2   He'd quit his job if he _____ (won) the lottery.

3   He _____ (go) home if he hadn't found another £20 in his wallet.

4   If you weren't so mean, you _____ (be) more popular.

5   I _____ (not mind) if my wife earned a higher salary than me.

4 Pronunciation – schwa /ə/ *3 points*

Underline the vowels that are pronounced using a schwa.

1   A fool and his money are soon parted.

2   The love of money is the root of all evil.

3   Money doesn't grow on trees.

5 Vocabulary – money expressions *4 points*

Complete the sentences with an appropriate word.

1   Gerry is the main bread _____ in our family.

2   I'm saving this money for a _____ day.

3   Yesterday I _____ out on some new clothes.

4   Sorry, I can't lend you any money. I'm completely _____ .

6 Linking words *6 points*

Complete the text using the linking words in the box.

by that time   during   as soon as   then   while   until

The first thing I did (1) _____ I inherited all the money was to leave my job. (2) _____ I took a trip around the world (3) _____ my newly-appointed assistant looked for a suitable castle in Scotland for me. (4) _____ my trip I met a diamond exporter. He persuaded me to invest a lot of my money in his business. It wasn't (5) _____ I was back in England, however, and hadn't heard from him in ages, that I realised that I had lost my fortune. But (6) _____ there was nothing I could do about it. Luckily my old boss let me have my old job back.

37

4 *Body* Overview

The topic of this unit is the body and health. The grammar focus is on phrasal verbs. The function of giving and receiving advice is also focused on.

Students start by reading conversations and identifying what is wrong with one of the speakers. They complete the conversations with suitable advice and practise using intonation to sound sympathetic.

A quiz introduces the topic of healthy lifestyles and this is followed by practice in giving and evaluating advice on taking care of your health.

Students learn several idioms using parts of the body and practise using them in conversations.

They then read about various diets and listen to two people talking about the diets they followed in order to lose weight for a special occasion.

In the next section, students do comprehension work on a fairly serious text on the difficulties of giving up smoking.

Finally, students examine in detail the use of phrasal verbs from the reading text and read some jokes whose humour depends on misinterpretation of the meaning of phrasal verbs.

Section	Aims	What the students are doing
Close up page 34–35	*Conversation skills*: expressing sympathy and giving advice	Matching conversations with ailments.
		Completing conversations by giving suitable advice.
		Practising sounding sympathetic.
	Listening skills: listening for detail	Listening to find if the advice given is similar to yours.
You're the expert page 35	*Conversation skills*: fluency work	Discussing healthy lifestyles.
		Answering a quiz.
	Listening skills: listening for detail	Listening to an expert on health and nutrition.
Close up page 36	*Functions*: recommendations	Giving and evaluating advice.
	Writing skills: letter writing	Writing a reply to a letter soliciting advice.
Body language page 37	*Listening skills*: listening for detail	Listening to a conversation and underlining what is different on the tapescript.
	Lexis: body idioms	Matching body idioms to their meanings.
		Finding more expressions using parts of the body.
	Conversation skills: fluency work	Describing people using body idioms.
		Writing conversations using body idioms.
Shape your body! page 38	*Reading skills*: reading for detail	Reading about various diets.
	Listening skills: listening for specific information; note-taking	Listening to two people talking about diets.
		Taking notes on what the speakers say.
I will quit. Soon page 39–40	*Reading skills*: scanning	Scanning an article about giving up smoking for specific information.
Close up pages 40–41	*Grammar*: phrasal verbs	Finding phrasal verbs in a text and using them to complete sentences.
		Matching phrasal verbs with their meanings.
		Reading some jokes whose humour depends on phrasal verbs.

4 Body *Teacher's notes*

Books closed. Make a worksheet with the following gapped sentences (or write them on the board / display them on an overhead projector). Ask the students to read them and to guess the numbers or percentages that should complete them. Allow them to discuss their answers in pairs or small groups. If you prefer, you could give them the answers (jumbled) and let them decide which one goes in each gap.

Check answers and see if anybody guessed any correctly. Initiate a discussion on which were the most surprising facts.

In the course of a lifetime, the average person ...

a)   spends _____ years eating.

b)   consumes _____ eggs and _____ kilos of chocolate.

c)   grows _____ metres of finger nails and _____ kilometres of hair on the head.

d)   talks on the phone for _____ years.

e)   only falls in love _____ .

f)   walks _____ kilometres.

g)   knows _____ people by name and calls _____ of them friends.

h)   lives for _____ years and has _____ children and _____ grandchildren.

i)   has a _____ chance of remaining married to the same person for the rest of their life.

a)	three and a half
b)	7,300; 160
c)	28; 725
d)	two and a half
e)	twice
f)	22,000
g)	2,000; 150
h)	79; 2; 4
i)	60%

Close up (p 34)

Books closed. Ask students to work in pairs and tell their partner about the last time they felt unwell. They should say why they felt unwell and what they did to make themselves feel better.

Sympathy & advice

1   Students read the conversations and the items in the table and decide what is wrong with the person in each conversation. Check answers with the class.

A	Bob's got a terrible hangover.
B	Dana's got a twisted ankle.
C	Ed's got a sore throat.
D	Greg's got really bad sunburn.
E	Jane's got a splitting headache.
F	Lisa's got dreadful hay fever.

2   Pairwork. Students read the conversations again and decide what advice the friend gives. They complete the friends' final sentences with suitable pieces of advice.

If some students finish before the others, encourage them to practise the conversations aloud.

3   🔲 **19 SB p 148**

Play the recording for students to listen to and see if the advice is similar to theirs. Ask them if they have ever tried any of the remedies suggested and whether they worked or not.

🔲 **19**

(A = Ann; B = Bob; C = Chris; D = Dana; E = Ed; F = Fran; G = Greg; H = Helen; I = Ian; J = Jane; K = Keith; L = Lisa)

A

A: *Oh dear – you look like death warmed up. Heavy night last night?*

B: *Yeah – good party, but I feel terrible.*

A: *Oh well, if you hadn't drunk so much you wouldn't be feeling so bad now, would you? Anyway, listen, I'll give you my secret cure: get a couple of raw eggs, mix them up in a cup, add a bit of chilli sauce and a pinch of salt, and drink it down in one go.*

B: *Ugh – that would just make me sick.*

A: *Yes, I know. But then you'd feel better, wouldn't you?*

B

C: *Why are you walking like that?*

D: *My ankle's killing me!*

C: *Oh dear, you poor thing! If you ask me, you need to lie down and put some ice on it to keep the swelling down.*

C

E: *Ugh! I can't swallow anything.*

F: *Oh yes, I know what you mean. I was the same last week. I could only eat ice cream!*

E: So, what did you do?

F: Well, you could try this. Chop up some ginger and put it in boiling water with some honey and lemon. Drink it as hot as you can.

E: Does it work?

F: Well, it makes you feel better, but it's probably a good idea to take some aspirin too.

D

G: Don't touch my back!

H: Why? What's up?

G: I wanted to get a tan quickly so I didn't bother to put any suntan lotion on.

H: Oh well, it serves you right then, doesn't it?

G: It really stings.

H: Okay, take your shirt off. I'll put some after-sun lotion on it.

E

I: When did it start?

J: After I'd been playing computer games for about seven hours. I feel as if my head's going to explode!

I: Oh well, you've only got yourself to blame, haven't you?

J: I know, I know. But I've taken aspirin, and it hasn't worked.

I: Well, you could try putting your hands over your eyes and leaving them there for about five minutes. That usually works for me, particularly if it's been brought on by sitting in front of the computer for too long.

F

K: Have you got a cold?

L: No, I'm all right – I always get a streaming nose and red eyes at this time of the year.

K: That must be awful. If I were you, I'd try acupuncture. My sister used to suffer terribly, but then she had three sessions of acupuncture, and that was it.

L: Really? Can you find out who she saw?

Sounding sympathetic (p 35)

1 Students work individually to mark the sentences *S* or *U*. Allow them to compare answers in pairs if they wish, before checking answers with the class.

a) U b) S c) S d) U e) U f) S

2 **20 SB p 35**
Pairwork. Play the recording for students to mark the stressed words and take note of the intonation. They can then practise saying the sentences in pairs, trying to sound sympathetic or unsympathetic.

(The stressed words are underlined.)

a) Oh <u>well</u>, if you hadn't <u>drunk</u> so <u>much</u> you wouldn't be <u>feeling</u> so <u>bad</u> <u>now</u>, <u>would</u> you?

b) Oh <u>dear</u>, you <u>poor</u> <u>thing</u>.

c) Oh <u>yes</u> , I <u>know</u> what you <u>mean</u>.

d) Oh <u>well</u>, it <u>serves</u> you <u>right</u> then, <u>doesn't</u> it?

e) Oh <u>well</u>, you've only got <u>yourself</u> to <u>blame</u>, <u>haven't</u> you?

f) That must be <u>awful</u>.

3 Pairwork. Students turn to their respective pages and take turns reading out problems and responding to their partner's problems with sympathy and advice.

4 Pairwork. Students discuss whether they have actually experienced any of the problems listed in 3 and, if so, what they did about it. Focus students' attention on sounding sympathetic when they are listening to each other.

You're the expert (p 35)

1 Books closed. Write 'How do you stay in good shape?' on the board and elicit as many responses as possible. Write them on the board and leave them there as reference for the next stage.

Groupwork. Students discuss the statements and decide if there are any that they agree with.

2 Pairwork. Students do the quiz individually and then compare results with a partner. Do not check answers at this stage.

3 📼 **21 SB p 148**
Play the recording for students to check their answers. Ask them if they are surprised by any of the answers.

1 c   2 a   3 b   4 a   5 b   6 c

📼 **21**

Liz Hartley

Okay, let's see how you got on with the Body knowledge quiz.

Number 1, the aerobic system is the heart, lungs and blood circulation. It's important to do aerobic exercise regularly, because it gets more oxygen into your blood and gets your heart pumping.

Yes, number two, the 'happy hormones'. These are endorphins, and they're the reason you feel so high when you've had a good work-out. It's a good idea to do exercise when you're feeling run down or stressed. The exercise releases these endorphins, and you end up feeling much better than before. It's the same feeling you get when you fall in love – but just doing exercise is probably less complicated.

A balanced diet, number three – um (b) is the correct answer here. You need to have a combination of carbohydrates, proteins and fats in your diet.

On the other hand, it's best not to include sugar and caffeine in your diet. They're just life's little luxuries, and they're not very good for you. You don't have to give them up completely, but you ought to cut down on them.

Okay, where were we? Ah yes, number 4 – for keeping supple, (a) is the correct answer. Obviously all these sports are really good for you, but if we're talking about improving the suppleness of your body, then you definitely need to do something like yoga, where you get a lot of stretching.

Right, number 5. If you exercise for twenty minutes three times a week, you're doing very well. One hour three times a week is fine, but you shouldn't overdo it – an hour every day is too much, except for professionals, of course. It's not a good idea to take it all too seriously, because that takes all the pleasure out of it.

And finally number 6. Stamina comes from practice, so you need to exercise regularly. Fruit's good for you, but it doesn't build up stamina – it has other benefits. Which is more than I can say for coffee – don't drink too much of it. It's poison!

Well that's it. But I'd just like to add a last piece of advice – try not to take it all too seriously. The more you enjoy what you're doing, the better you'll feel. So find the kind of exercise that suits you, and enjoy yourself!

Close up (p 36)

Recommendations

1 Students work individually to complete the sentences from memory. Play the recording again for them to check their answers.

a) important, do
b) idea, do
c) need, have
d) best, to
e) don't, to, ought, cut
f) need, do
g) shouldn't
h) not, good, to
i) Don't
j) Try, to

2 Pairwork. Students discuss which piece of advice they think is most sensible and which they would find most difficult to follow. You could have a class vote on both questions. Ask students if they have ever tried to follow any of this advice and how successful they were.

3 Pairwork. Students read the letter and write down their

suggestions. They then report back to the class. Ask the class to discuss which suggestions they think are best.

4 Students can work individually or in pairs to write their replies to the letter. Direct their attention to the language reference on this page which gives them some useful language.

Follow up activity

In pairs/small groups, students create a problem and write it on a piece of paper. When they have finished, they pass their paper to the next pair/group to their left. That pair/group then writes some advice (on a separate piece of paper) and passes the problem left. This should continue until three separate pieces of advice have been written for the same problem. The original problem should then be handed back to each group along with the three pieces of advice from the other groups. Each group selects what they feel to be the best piece of advice to display on the class wall along with their problem.

Body language (p 37)

Idioms

1 📼 **22 SB p 149**

Students read the conversation as they listen to the recording. Go through the instructions first so that they understand that the recording is slightly different from the conversation in the book. They should listen out for the differences and underline them. Check answers with the class before going on to 2.

(L = Laura; P = Phil)

L: Hey, Phil, how are you doing?

P: Oh hi, Laura – not too bad thanks. How are you?

L: Oh, extremely busy as usual. I'm on my way to my third meeting today. How's that lovely girlfriend of yours?

P: Oh, we split up three weeks ago. She's on holiday with her new boyfriend.

L: Oh no – trust me to say something to make you feel worse. I'm really sorry.

P: No, it's okay. I need to talk about it.

L: Who's her new boyfriend?

P: It's her boss. You wouldn't know him. He's not from around here.

L: What kind of work does he do?

P: I don't know really. He seems to be involved in a lot of things. He owns several companies anyway, including the one Mandy was working for.

L: Oh Phil, I don't know what to say.

P: Yeah – it's hard. I mean, we were supposed to be going on holiday together in a couple of weeks.

L: So, what are you going to do?

P: I don't know – I haven't decided yet. I might go anyway, or I might not feel like it when the time comes. I don't know. I'll just have to <u>see how I feel at the time</u>.

L: Look Phil, I'm afraid I've got to run – but if you need <u>some sympathy</u>, you know where to find me.

P: Thanks, Laura – I'll be fine.

2 Students replace the underlined phrases with idioms from the box. Do not check answers at this stage, but allow students to compare with a partner if they wish.

3 Play the recording again for students to check their answers.

22

(L = Laura; P = Phil)

L: *Hey, Phil, how are you doing?*

P: *Oh hi, Laura – not too bad thanks. How are you?*

L: *Oh, <u>up to my eyes in work</u> as usual. I'm on my way to my third meeting today. How's that lovely girlfriend of yours?*

P: *Oh, we split up three weeks ago. She's on holiday with her new boyfriend.*

L: *Oh no – trust me to <u>put my foot in it</u>. I'm really sorry.*

P: *No, it's okay. I need to <u>get it off my chest</u>.*

L: *Who's her new boyfriend?*

P: *It's her boss. You wouldn't know him. He's <u>not from this neck of the woods</u>.*

L: *What kind of work does he do?*

P: *I don't know really. He seems to <u>have his fingers in a lot of pies</u>. He owns several companies anyway, including the one Mandy was working for.*

L: *Oh Phil, I don't know what to say.*

P: *Yeah – it's hard. I mean, we were supposed to be going on holiday together in a couple of weeks.*

L: *So, what are you going to do?*

P: *I don't know – I haven't <u>made up my mind yet</u>. I might go anyway, or I might not feel like it when the time comes. I don't know. I'll just have to <u>play it by ear</u>.*

L: *Look Phil, I'm afraid I've got to run – but if you need <u>a shoulder to cry on</u>, you know where to find me.*

P: *Thanks, Laura – I'll be fine.*

4 Pairwork. Students read the list and take turns to tell each other about someone they know who fits the descriptions.

5 Pairwork. Students decide on their roles and look up expressions using their respective body parts. Ask several pairs to report back to the class on the expressions they have found.

Possible answers

Student A

nose: poke your nose into; look down your nose; pay through the nose; put someone's nose out of joint; under someone's nose

brain: have something on the brain

hand: have your hands full; by hand; be a good hand at doing something; be an old hand at doing something; give someone a big hand; give/lend a hand; get out of hand; have a matter well in hand; at first hand; at hand; at second hand; change hands; get/keep your hand in; give somebody a free hand; be hand in glove with somebody; hand in hand; to have a hand in something; on hand; on the one hand / on the other hand; play into somebody's hands; to hand; turn your hand to; wait on somebody hand and foot

eye: in the eyes of; keep an eye on; keep an eye out for; keep your eyes open; see eye to eye; under/before your very eyes; up to your eyes in; with your eyes open; open-eyed

Student B

leg: on your last legs; pull someone's leg; stretch you legs

tongue: hold your tongue; with your tongue in your cheek

head: take/get something into your head; put our heads together; above/over your head; bring something to a head; come to a head; go to somebody's head; have your head in the clouds; head over heels; keep your head; not be able to make head or tail of something; off your head

foot: set foot in; find your feet; get/have cold feet; have one foot in the grave; on foot; put a foot wrong; put your best foot forward; put your feet up; put your foot down; put your foot in it; be run off your feet

6 Pairwork. Students work together on their conversations using the expressions they found in 5. Go round giving help where necessary. Ask several pairs to act out their conversations for the class.

Shape your body! (p 38)

Reading & listening

1 Pairwork. Students take turns asking and answering the questions. They then report back to the class.

2 Give students plenty of time to read the article and find the answers. Allow them to compare answers in pairs before checking with the class.

a) Grapefruit diet

b) System S diet

c) No-carbohydrate diet

d) F-plan diet

e) Cabbage soup diet

f) Hay diet

3 🔲 **23 SB p 149**

Go through the instructions with the class, then play the recording. Students listen and decide what each special occasion was. Check answers with the class.

Sam: a kick-boxing tournament

Catherine: her wedding (or more precisely getting into her wedding dress)

🔲 **23**

Sam

(I = Interviewer; S = Sam)

I: Congratulations on winning the tournament, Sam. How do you feel?

S: Oh, great!

I: Are you going to celebrate?

S: Definitely. I've been training non-stop for ages and I need a good night out.

I: How do you train for a kick-boxing tournament like this?

S: Basically, you have to live like a monk for weeks ...

I: Really? Aren't you allowed to go out?

S: Yes, actually you can go out, but you can't drink or smoke and you have to be in bed by midnight.

I: I guess that's quite difficult for a young guy like yourself. What other sacrifices do you have to make?

S: Well, obviously you have train every day, and the main thing for kick-boxing is to build up your stamina – so while I'm training I have to be quite strict with my diet.

I: So what do you eat?

S: Um, the first thing is cutting down on fat – no crisps or burgers. I'm not supposed to eat butter, but that's really hard because I really love it. Oh, and I mustn't drink too much caffeine.

I: And what sort of things are good for you?

S: High-fibre food like brown rice and vegetables. Cranberry juice is good – loads and loads of fluid. That's really important.

I: And what about protein?

S: Yeah, of course that's important, but meat tends to be very fatty – I try to stick to fish. Mushrooms are really good – I eat lots of mushrooms. But carbohydrates are as important as protein because I need the energy. I don't want to end up with enormous muscles.

I: Talking of muscles, do you work out?

S: Of course – that's part of the training. I work out every day, but I do quite a lot of aerobic exercise and not too much weight-lifting. For kick-boxing you have to increase your energy levels.

I: What are you going to have for dinner now the competition's over?

S: Steak and chips with loads of bread and butter, Coke to drink, followed by apple pie and cream. And a double expresso. No problem.

I: A well-earned treat. Enjoy it! Thank you, Sam Davidson, the new kick-boxing champion – and now back to the studio.

Catherine

(C = Catherine; M = Mike)

M: Catherine, you look great in these photos.

C: Oh, thanks. I had to go through hell to get into that wedding dress.

M: What do you mean?

C: It was too small.

M: Why didn't you get one your size?

C: Oh, it was my grandmother's – my mother wore it on her wedding day, and I really wanted to wear it on mine.

M: Oh, I can see why – it's gorgeous. But the waist is minute!

C: Tell me about it. I suffered for six months so I could wear it.

M: How did you do it?

C: Oh, well, you know this diet that all the Hollywood actors are doing?

M: No – I thought they just had plastic surgery every time their body needed reshaping.

C: Well, they probably do that as well – but there's this new diet. I don't think it's very healthy if you do it for a long time, but it really works.

M: Is it the diet where you think of all the food you love and avoid it for six months?

C: No – actually, it's amazing. Believe it or not, you can eat things like, em, roast chicken and steak and eggs and bacon, but you just can't eat any carbohydrates with it.

M: No bread.

C: No.

M: What about pasta?

C: No.

M: Oh, I couldn't live without pasta.

C: Mm, it was hard – I was dying for a nice plate of spaghetti.

M: Did you have to exercise?

C: Well, you know me – I'm not exactly sportswoman of the year. But I wanted to get rid of my stomach so I had to do sit-ups every morning. Nightmare!

M: How much did you lose?

> C: *To be honest, I have no idea – the important thing to me was that I could put that dress on and look good in it.*
>
> M: *Are you still dieting then?*
>
> C: *No way – I love my food and dieting is so boring. Hopefully, I won't need to wear the wedding dress again anyway!*

4 Play the recording again. Students listen and make notes. When you have played the recording for the second time, ask if they can now complete the table. If they can't, play the recording again. Allow students to compare notes in pairs before checking with the class.

> Sam wasn't allowed: to drink or smoke; crisps, burgers, butter; too much caffeine
>
> Sam was allowed: to go out; brown rice and vegetables; cranberry juice
>
> Sam had to: live like a monk; be in bed by midnight; train every day; be strict with his diet; drink lots of fluids; eat carbohydrates and protein; increase his energy levels
>
> Catherine wasn't allowed: carbohydrates; bread; pasta
>
> Catherine was allowed: roast chicken and steak; eggs and bacon
>
> Catherine had to: go through hell; do sit-ups every morning

5 Students match the diets in 1 to the diets described by Sam and Catherine. Check answers with the class.

> Sam: F-plan diet
>
> Catherine: No-carbohydrate diet

6 Whole class. Students discuss which of the diets they would find hardest to follow. If they wish, they could tell the class about any diets they have tried.

I will quit. Soon (p 39)

Reading

You might like to begin by asking students about their attitudes to smoking. Do they, or have they ever smoked? Why did they start? Have they ever tried to give up? Is smoking in public places considered acceptable in their country or countries? Is there anywhere it is not acceptable to smoke?

1 Students can work individually or in pairs to think up their three answers to each point. Get feedback from the class.

2 Go through the points that students are looking for before they start reading. Give them plenty of time to read the article before checking answers. Then ask them whether they think the writer is likely to give up and why/why not.

> a) He's getting old and he can't keep harming himself by smoking. He's losing control. It's not just a 'habit'. He's 'hooked'.
>
> b) It's never let him down. It's never abandoned him on lonely, desperate nights. It clears his head and helps him to think. It has started conversations. It has driven away annoying people. It helps him celebrate victories, get over losses, comfort the comfortless. It also chases away mosquitoes.
>
> c) He has been to see Shubentsov, who is known around the world for curing smokers of their habit, using a mystical method.

3 Students find words and expressions in the text to replace the underlined ones in the sentences. Check answers with the class.

> a) feel the urge
>
> b) picked up
>
> c) struggle
>
> d) lets me down
>
> e) get over
>
> f) claim to
>
> g) 'm hooked
>
> h) give up

Close up (p 40)

Phrasal verbs

1 Ask the class for a few examples of phrasal verbs and write them on the board. Make sure that some of them are transitive and some are intransitive and explain the difference. Elicit sentences using the verbs on the board and ensure students are using them correctly. Point out how the dictionaries the students use indicate whether a verb is transitive or intransitive.

Students then turn back to the text on giving up smoking and find and underline eleven phrasal verbs. They then decide which one is intransitive.

> hopped down   picked ... up   picked up
> have let ... down   get over   has driven away
> chases away   give up   lighting up
> call ... back   put ... down
>
> *hopped down* is intransitive.

2 Students work individually to complete the sentences. Check answers with the class.

> a) picked it up
>
> b) lets him down

c) drives them away

d) chases them away

e) call him back

f) put it down

3 Pairwork. Students discuss the questions. They can check their answers with the Language reference section on page 41 before you check answers with the class.

a) Transitive.

b) Separable.

c) You must put it between the verb and the particle.

4 Whole class. Students can do this matching orally.

it dawned on him – it became clear to him

Step on it! – Hurry up!

a feeling came over me – a feeling affected me strongly

we're looking into it – we're investigating it

you can count on it – you can depend on it

we saw through them – we weren't deceived by them

5 Give students time to replace the underlined words and to consider why the jokes are funny. (They all depend on a literal interpretation of the verbs, which the speakers are using idiomatically.) Allow them to discuss this in pairs if they wish.

a) are looking into it

b) can see through them

c) step on it

d) count on it

e) come over you

f) dawned on him

6 Pairwork. Students look back at the verbs in 5 and discuss the questions.

a) Transitive.

b) Not separable.

c) You must put it after the particle.

7 Give students time to consult their own dictionaries to find out the answer to this question. If they don't all have dictionaries, put them in pairs or groups.

8 Students work individually to write their five sentences. They can then compare them with a partner.

Test

Scoring: one point per correct answer unless otherwise indicated.

1 1 need, be

2 Don't do

3 not, good idea

4 important

5 don't have

6 shouldn't

7 not, smoke

8 try not

2 (2 points per correct answer)

1 sunburn

2 headache

3 hay fever

4 ankle

5 hangover

6 throat

3 (2 points per correct answer)

1 Oh dear

2 Have you tried

3 shouldn't

4 Poor you

5 were you

4 1 pick up

2 step on it

3 looking into

4 driving away

5 get over

6 put down

7 dawned on

8 give up

9 count on

10 lets ... down

4 Body Test

Name: **Total:** _____ /40

1 Instructions & recommendations *8 points*

Complete the sentences.

1   You'll n_____ to b_____ fitter if you want to play.

2   D_____ d_____ exercise without warming up first.

3   It's n_____ a g_____ i_____ to eat too much red meat.

4   It's really i_____ to eat a balanced diet.

5   You d_____ h_____ to do a lot to stay healthy.

6   She told me I s_____ overdo it at the gym.

7   It's best n_____ to s_____ cigarettes.

8   I t_____ n_____ to eat sweets, but it's very difficult!

2 Vocabulary – the body *12 points*

Complete the sentences with an appropriate word.

1   I'm putting on lots of sunscreen. I don't want to get _____ on the beach this year.

2   I've had a splitting _____ all day. I'm going to have to take an aspirin.

3   She gets really bad _____ every summer, especially when they're cutting the grass.

4   While James was playing football he fell awkwardly and twisted his _____ .

5   Paula was celebrating last night with a few drinks and she's got a bit of a _____ this morning.

6   I've got such a sore _____ . I can't eat or drink anything without it hurting.

3 Language of sympathy & advice *10 points*

Complete the dialogue with the appropriate expressions.

A: I'm really having trouble sleeping recently.

B: (1) O_____ , d_____ . (2) H_____ y_____ t_____ *Sweet Dreams*, that relaxing music CD? It's very good.

A: I usually just read a book, hoping it will send me to sleep.

B: You (3) s_____ do that! It just stimulates the brain.

A: I know. Last night I was reading a crime thriller and I was awake all night thinking about it.

B: (4) P _____ y_____ . It doesn't sound much fun. If I (5) w_____ y_____ , I'd put the CD on when you go to bed, and you'll be asleep before you know it.

4 Phrasal verbs *10 points*

Complete the sentences with the correct form of the following phrasal verbs.

put down	get over	pick up	look into	drive away
count on	dawn on	step on it	give up	let down

1   Josy found it quite easy to _____ the language when she was living in Spain.

2   You'd better _____ , otherwise we'll be late.

3   The government are _____ the problem of rising crime.

4   You're _____ the customers with these high prices.

5   I still can't _____ how well I did in the exams.

6   Will you _____ that book for a minute and come and help me in the kitchen!

7   It suddenly _____ Steve that Mandy had been right all along.

8   I've tried to _____ eating snacks between meals, but I can't.

9   You can always _____ your best friend to help out if you're in trouble.

10   This car is really reliable. It never _____ me _____ .

5 Ritual Overview

The topic of this unit is rituals – from the small series of actions that people believe will bring luck in certain situations to the major rituals of society, such as weddings. The main grammar focus is on verbs which can take either the *to*-infinitive or the *-ing* form with different meanings, and present and past habits.

The first section is about rituals associated with football. Students read an extract from Nick Hornby's novel, *Fever Pitch*, in which he describes the strange rituals he and his fellow football supporters have adopted which they think might bring their team luck. Students discuss their own personal rituals.

They then look at verbs which can take either the *to*-infinitive or the *-ing* form and see how the meaning changes according to which structure is used.

The next section contains a 'thought conversation' between a married couple who are having dinner on their wedding anniversary. They have very different attitudes to their night out and students choose appropriate verb patterns to complete their thoughts.

Students then listen to a woman talking about her father's obsession with his car and study the structures used to talk about present and past habits. They also practise the intonation used to convey annoyance.

Wedding rituals around the world are discussed next. Students then look at some quotations about marriage and make up some of their own.

The final section looks at the rituals associated with greeting people and saying goodbye.

Section	Aims	What the students are doing
Football mad! page 42–43	*Lexis*: football vocabulary	Testing knowledge of football vocabulary and answering questions about it.
	Reading skills: reading for gist	Reading an extract from a novel and choosing the sentence that best describes the author's attitude to football.
Close up page 44–45	*Grammar*: verb + either *to*-infinitive or *-ing* form	Extending the study of *to*-infinitive and *-ing* form by looking at verbs which can take either, and examining how the meaning changes.
Anniversary night out page 46	*Lexis*: verb + *to*-infinitive, verb + *-ing* form, verb + either *to*-infinitive or *-ing* form	Reading the differing thoughts of two people having dinner together on their wedding anniversary. Choosing the correct verb pattern.
A man and his car page 47	*Listening skills*: listening for detail	Listening to a girl talking about her father's obsession with his car, and linking phrases. Using expressions from the listening text to complete sentences.
Close up pages 47–49	*Grammar*: present and past habits; stress and intonation to convey annoyance	Practising using the correct verb structures to describe present and past habits. Practising using stress and intonation to convey annoyance.
The big day page 49	*Listening skills*: listening for detail	Discussing wedding rituals and listening to people from different countries talking about them.
	Conversation skills: fluency work	Anecdote: talking about a wedding.
Marriage is … page 50	*Writing skills*: writing sentences following given criteria	Choosing appropriate endings to quotations about marriage. Writing 'quotations' about marriage following given criteria.
Small talk page 51	*Speaking and writing skills*: jigsaw dictation	Taking turns to dictate and write down parts of a conversation.
	Lexis: expressions for saying goodbye	Completing a conversation with various expressions for saying goodbye.

5 *Ritual* Teacher's notes

Football mad! (p 42)

Books closed. Draw a horizontal line on the board. At the left-hand end write *I hate it*, a little further along *I don't like it*, then *I'm not interested in it*, then *I'm interested in it*, then *I really like it*, and at the right-hand end write *I'm mad about it*. Get the class to ask you *How do you feel about football?* Answer with one of the sentences on the board. Ask students to copy the diagram into their books and write the names of other students beside the different sentences according to what they predict the other students think of football. Give students the opportunity to check their predictions.

Lexis (p 42)

Whole class. Ask students to read the definition of *ritual* in the margin. Then focus attention on the football photograph at the bottom of the page. Ask them to say what the connection is. What aspects of going to a football match are a ritual?

1 Students work individually to complete the questions. Check answers with the class.

> a) support   b) colours   c) players   d) stadium
> e) lose   f) won   g) scored   h) match

2 Students interested in football can answer the questions themselves. Others should mingle round the classroom finding someone to answer them. Get feedback from the class.

3 Whole class. Elicit responses to the first question and write them on the board. Encourage students to say whether they regard this kind of behaviour as positive or negative.

Then ask them if they know anybody who is obsessed with football. If they do, ask them to describe this person's behaviour. If the person described is in the class and is not embarrassed about this, encourage them to give their reactions and talk about their obsession with football.

Optional activity

Focus students' attention on the photograph on page 42. Encourage any students who have admitted to being obsessed with football to describe the photograph. Ask them to say what they think is happening or has just happened and how they would feel if they were members of the crowd.

Reading (p 43)

Books closed. Ask if anyone has read the book *Fever Pitch* by Nick Hornby or has seen the film. Encourage anyone who has to talk to the class about it.

1 Whole class. Read the instructions with the class and direct their attention to the information abut Nick Hornby. Then give them plenty of time to read the text and decide which sentence best describes the writer's attitude.

> d)   He's absolutely mad about it.

2 Whole class. Ask students what the writer means by rituals (actions that a person does, believing them to be in some way 'lucky' and likely to cause a desired outcome). Give them time to decide how many rituals are mentioned and which one has been most successful. You might also like to ask whether the students believe it has really been successful and to initiate a discussion on whether they have ever performed certain rituals in the hope of causing something to happen.

> Eleven rituals are mentioned.
> The sugar mouse ritual was the only successful ritual.

3 Whole class. Elicit opinions on the person in the text. Encourage students to describe anyone they know who is similar.

4 Pairwork. Students can discuss rituals they themselves perform in the given situations or rituals they have heard of other people performing. Encourage them to report anything interesting back to the class.

Close up (p 44)

Verbs + *to*-infinitive & -*ing* form

1 Check that students are familiar with the *to*-infinitive and the -*ing* form by asking them to produce example sentences using each of them.

Students then work individually to complete the texts. Do not check answers at this stage, but allow students to compare with a partner if they wish.

2 🔲 **24 SB p 149**
Play the recording for students to listen to and check their answers.

> Terry
> 1   watching
> 2   equalizing
> 3   believing
> Dawn
> 1   to set
> 2   to buy
> 3   to programme

24

Terry, a Manchester United supporter

I remember watching Man Utd against Bayern Munich in the Champions League final. I'll never forget Sheringham equalizing in the 89th minute. Then Solsjkar scored the winner two minutes later in injury time. It was incredible! With ten minutes to go I had already stopped believing it was possible to win, but Man Utd just never gave up!

Dawn, a Chelsea supporter

If I've forgotten to set the alarm clock, it's always a rush. I have breakfast quickly, put on my Chelsea shirt and leave the house. I can walk to the ground from where I live, and I always stop to buy a newspaper and get the latest team news. Three hours before kick-off and the atmosphere is already building. It's a great day out – the best moment in the week. If I remember to programme the video, then I can watch the whole match again when I get home. Magic!

3 Draw students' attention to the fact that the same verbs, *remember, forget* and *stop*, are used in both texts before the *to*-infinitive and *-ing* forms. Elicit which structure is used for a–d.

> a)   remember / (never) forget + *-ing* form
> b)   remember / forget + *to*-infinitive
> c)   stop + *-ing* form
> d)   stop + *to*-infinitive

Refer students to the Language reference section on page 45 for more information about these forms.

Optional activity

Ask students to write pairs of sentences of their own using *remember, forget* and *stop*, showing the difference in meaning between the *to*-infinitive and the *-ing* form.

4   **25 SB p 149**

Play the recording for students to listen to and underline the verb structures that Mark uses.

> 1 going   2 to think   3 being   4 to arrive
> 5 seeing

25

Mark and Tim, Tottenham supporters

When I was about fourteen, I tried going to football matches for a while. All my friends did it, so I joined in just to be like them. I liked to think I was one of the lads – you know how it is. I loved being part of a big crowd, but apart from that I was never really that interested, and as I got older I remember

thinking what a waste of time it all was. Anyway, after my third season I stopped going.

But now, my nine-year-old son is football mad, so I've started going again. He likes to arrive really early at the stadium to get a good place, so I'm spending more time there than ever! I love seeing his face when they score, but although I try to show how interested I am, it's no good. I can still think of a hundred things I'd rather be doing on a Saturday than standing around watching a football match.

5 Students look at the text again and find examples for each of the concepts. This can be done orally as a whole-class activity.

> a) 6   b) 1   c) 3, 5   d) 2, 4

6 Students complete the statements. Allow them to compare answers in pairs before checking with the class.

> a) playing   b) to do   c) telling   d) to do
> e) to pick up   f) sleeping   g) windsurfing
> h) to learn   i) to keep   j) driving

7 Pairwork. Students work individually to rewrite any sentences that are untrue for them. They then compare their sentences with a partner and discuss any differences.

Anniversary night out (p 46)

Books closed. Write *A night to remember* on the board and ask the class if anyone knows or can guess what it means. The expression usually refers to a night that is memorable because it is very enjoyable. Ask students for examples of things that would make an evening out memorable for them – these could be very good things or very bad things.

Lexis (p 46)

Pairwork. First read the introduction with the whole class to establish the situation. Students then decide whether they are going to be Chris or Shirley. They work individually to complete their character's thoughts. They can refer back to the verb patterns on page 45 if they are still unsure of the use of *to*-infinitives and *-ing* forms. They then compare their results and decide whether the evening will be a success or not. Finally they categorise the verb patterns. Check answers with the class.

> a)
> *Chris*
> 1 bringing   2 telling   3 looking   4 to have
> 5 spending   6 picking up   7 to look   8 driving
> 9 going   10 being
> *Shirley*
> 1 to bring   2 to tell   3 to look   4 having
> 5 to spend   6 to pick   7 looking   8 to drive
> 9 to go   10 to be

b)

The expression 'a night to remember' usually refers to a night that is memorable because it is very enjoyable. It seems likely that this will not be enjoyable because the two people are looking at the evening from widely different points of view.

c)

Verbs + *to*-infinitive: manage, deserve, intend, want, expect

Verbs + *-ing* form: couldn't help, imagine, enjoy, fancy, can't stand

Verbs + *to*-infinitive or *-ing* form: remember, forget, hate, stop, regret*, like

(*In the conversation only *regret* + *-ing* form is exemplified.)

A man and his car (p 47)

Listening

Books closed. Remind students that in an earlier section they read about a man who was obsessed with football. Ask for examples of other things that people can be obsessed with and write them on the board. Have a class discussion on whether men or women are more likely to be obsessed by the things suggested. Encourage students to give examples of people they know who are obsessed. Ask them if they think the people themselves would agree that they are obsessed or whether it is just the opinion of other people who don't share their interests.

1   ▭▭   **26 SB p 150**

Read the phrases with the whole class before you play the recording. Students then listen and link the phrases in A with those in B. Allow them to compare answers with a partner before checking with the class. Then ask students to say what Laura's father's rituals are.

> a) 5   b) 4   c) 1   d) 2   e) 6   f) 3

▭▭   **26**

My dad is the most ritualistic person I know, and many of his rituals involve his car.

We've never kept domestic animals in our house, but my father's car is as close as you'll get to the family pet. In fact, to be honest, the car probably gets better treatment and more affection than a pet would.

Each night, the car is tucked up in its garage under a cosy blanket. Nobody – but nobody – is allowed in the garage in case they accidentally brush against 'the precious one', causing who knows what damage.

When we were children, on the rare occasions when my dad would get the car out of the garage (for births, deaths, marriages and national disasters – and then only if the buses weren't running), we

would have to wear paper bags on our feet in case we had a sudden urge to vandalise the seats with our school shoes.

We would never be allowed to shut the car doors ourselves ... in case we banged them too hard, I suppose. I mean, three, five and seven-year-old children can do untold damage to a car by banging the door shut.

Nowadays, we don't have to wear paper bags on our feet, but the 'Starting the car and setting off' ritual has never changed.

He'll start the engine and then sit there for at least five minutes with the engine turning. As repulsive fumes pump out into the fresh country air, he'll take out his pipe, and start tapping out his last smoke. Then he'll take a pinch of Players Medium Navy Cut (no other tobacco will do), stuff it in the bowl and spend a minute or two patting it down. Next, he'll get out his box of matches and give it a shake. He always gives his matchbox a shake. The pipe won't light first go – he'll have several goes at it, and finally, when the tobacco takes, he'll puff and puff until the car is full of smoke. With visibility dangerously reduced and a carful of choking passengers, he'll take the hand-brake off and reverse out of the drive at hair-raising speed.

It isn't pleasant being a passenger, but we've always let him get away with this strange behaviour because he's the boss. None of us would dare to complain.

My father used to be a pilot in the Royal Air Force, and I often wonder whether he would indulge in this kind of ritual before take-off and whether his crew would let him get away with it because he was the boss. Probably.

2   Students work individually to decide whether the statements are true or false. They then compare answers with a partner before listening to the recording again.

> a) True   b) False   c) False   d) True   e) True

3   This could be done individually or orally with the whole class. Encourage the students to try to complete the whole exercise before turning to the tapescript.

> a)   as close as you'll get
>
> b)   tucked up
>
> c)   sudden urge
>
> d)   several goes
>
> e)   hair-raising speed
>
> f)   got away

Follow up activity

Students write their own sentences using the expressions in 3. However, they leave a gap where the expression should be and write it on the back of their paper. Holding their paper facing away from them (so that other students can read the gapped sentences), students move around the class reading and orally completing each other's sentences with an appropriate expression.

Close up (p 47)

Present & past habits

1 Pairwork. Students look at the extracts and discuss the questions. Check answers with the class. Refer students to the Language reference section on page 49 for more information about these structures.

> a) Present habits.
> b) *will ('ll)*
> c) An action.
> d) Many times.
> e) Typical.
> f) You will be describing past habits.

2 Students do the first part individually and then work in pairs to discuss their own family's morning routines. Make sure they understand that not all the verbs can be changed.

> 1   will get up
> 2   hates
> 3   'll have
> 4   's
> 5   won't usually get ready
> 6   likes
> 7   's got
> 8   'll always leave
> 9   will vary
> 10 'll usually depend

3 Pairwork. Students make sentences using an element from each of the three boxes. Go round offering help and encouragement and take note of any interesting things you hear which can be reported back to the class.

Annoying habits (p 48)

1 📼 **27 SB p 150**

Before you start the exercise, have a brainstorming session on what kinds of things would make a work-mate (or class-mate) annoying.

Students then complete the sentences with phrases from the box. Play the recording for them to listen to and check their answers.

> a)   's forever talking
> b)   will insist on opening
> c)   's always leaving

> d)   will go on about
> e)   's always telling
> f)   will keep using

📼 **27**

> a)   *I share an office with a woman who's forever talking to her boyfriend on the phone, blowing kisses and saying intimate things that I don't want to listen to. It really gets on my nerves!*
> b)   *She will insist on opening all the windows when she arrives in the morning, and then she complains it's freezing and puts the heating on full blast. The office is either freezing or boiling!*
> c)   *She's always leaving half finished cups of coffee around the desk – then I knock them over and it's my fault!*
> d)   *She will go on about her personal problems. Honestly, you'd think I was her therapist or something – I should charge her for my time!*
> e)   *She's always telling me what to do, which I resent. I mean, I was working here when she was still at school!*
> f)   *I've told her hundreds of times to get her own pencil sharpener and scissors, but she will keep using mine and not putting them back in their place. So when I need them I can never find them!*

2 Whole class. Elicit answers to the questions. Go through the Language reference section on page 49 with the students if they have difficulty with these structures.

> She uses: *forever/always* + present continuous; *will* + infinitive (without *to*); *will insist on* + *-ing* form; *will keep* + *-ing* form

3 Pairwork. Students discuss the habits described in 1 and decide which they would find the most annoying. When they have numbered them in order, see how many pairs in the class agree.

Sounding annoyed (p 48)

1 📼 **28 SB p 150**

Pairwork. Play the recording. Students listen and mark the stressed words, noting the woman's intonation. Then they take turns to say the sentences to each other, trying to sound annoyed.

📼 **28**

> a)   *She's <u>forever</u> <u>talking</u> to her <u>boyfriend</u> on the <u>phone</u>.*
> b)   *She <u>will</u> <u>insist</u> on opening <u>all</u> the <u>windows</u>.*
> c)   *She's <u>always</u> <u>leaving</u> <u>half-finished</u> <u>cups</u> of <u>coffee</u> <u>around</u> the desk.*

d) She _will_ _go_ _on_ about her _personal_ _problems_.

e) She's always telling me _what_ to _do_.

f) She _will_ _keep_ _using_ my pencil _sharpener_ and _scissors_.

2 Pairwork. Students take turns to describe the annoying habits of people they know. Encourage them to report any interesting information back to the class, paying particular attention to their stress and intonation.

The big day (p 49)

Books closed. Write the words _The big day_ in the centre of the board and ask students if they know what they refer to (a wedding day). Brainstorm words associated with weddings and add them to the board, building up a spidergram with different sections, eg food, people, clothes, place, etc. Encourage students to tell you, as they call out new words, which section to put them in.

Listening (p 49)

1 Groupwork. Students read the rituals and discuss whether they are common in their country or countries. They then try to decide what each ritual means.

a) The bride and groom cut the wedding cake together. This is supposed to symbolise the couple's commitment to working together through their married life.

b) This is supposed to symbolise the intention to share all worldly goods.

c) The guests intend to help the bride and groom set themselves up for their life together.

d) This is supposed to bring the bride and groom luck and ensure that they have children.

e) It is believed that holding a black umbrella over the bride's head as she leaves her home will protect her from bad luck.

f) It is believed that the person (usually a woman) who catches the bouquet will be the next one to get married.

2 ▭▭ **29 SB p 150**

Go through the questions with the class. Then play the recording. Students listen and make notes of their answers.

a) Rituals b, e, c.

b) coins – Spain; umbrella – Taiwan; money – Turkey

▭▭ **29**

1

(I = Interviewer; B = Belen)

I: _Tell me about weddings in your country._

B: _Well, in Spain, where I'm from, there is this ritual, er, that, er, happens after the rings have been exchanged between groom and bride. It is called las arras, and it consists of thirteen gold coins which, er, the groom puts in the bride's hands. Um, it symbolises their intention of, um, sharing everything: all the worldly goods they are going to receive together._

2

(I = Interviewer; N = Nerissa)

I: _Tell me about weddings in your country._

N: _Well, um, in Taiwan, um, we use a black umbrella to cover the bride's head, because we believe that it can protect the bride from the evil spirits. So normally there will be an elder person to hold the umbrella when she leaves her house to a groom's house._

I: _And will this bring her good luck as well?_

N: _Yes, it will prevent bad luck._

3

(I = Interviewer; C = Carmel)

I: _Tell me about wedding traditions in Turkey._

C: _Um, I'm not actually Turkish, but I'm married to a Turk. And, er, the weddings in Turkey are quite different to how they are in the UK. Um, there are a lot of people at the wedding. There are sometimes as many as four or five hundred guests, and one of the most interesting things, I think, about Turkish weddings, er, is the fact that, er, the guests at the wedding pin, um, gold, money, banknotes, on the, er, bride's and groom's, er, costumes, on their, er, on the bridegroom's suit and on the bride's dress. Um, I think, as, from what I can understand, that this money and gold is used to, er, by the bride and groom, to, er, to set themselves up for their new life together, er, living in their, er, new house, their new home, to buy things like a fridge, and, er, and other things they might need for their future life together._

Anecdote (p 49)

(See the Introduction on page 4 for more ideas on how to set up, monitor and repeat 'anecdotes'.)

Pairwork. Give students plenty of time to read the questions and decide what they are going to say. They then take turns to talk about a wedding. Encourage the listening partners to listen attentively and to ask appropriate questions at the end to elicit more information.

Marriage is ... (p 50)

1 Pairwork. Students discuss the quotations and decide which endings they think are best. Allow them to compare with other pairs before getting feedback from the class. Encourage students to say why they chose particular endings.

2 Students work individually to make their own endings for the quotations in 1. They can then compare with a partner or in groups.

3 Groupwork. First go through the instructions with the class. Make sure they understand that they can only use the words on the tiles, though they can use each one more than once. Students work together to make 'quotations' using the given criteria.

4 Groupwork. Groups compare 'quotations' with each other and discuss how many they agree and disagree with. You might like to ask the class to choose the best 'quotation' in each category.

Small talk (p 51)

Lexis

1   🔲 **30 SB p 150**

Pairwork. Students turn to their respective pages. They take turns to dictate and write down parts of a conversation. When they have finished, play the recording for them to check their answers.

Student A

a) Oh, not much. The usual.

b) Yes, it must be over a year.

c) Thank you. Give her mine.

d) How do you do.

Student B

a) I will.

b) You're welcome. You must come again soon.

c) I won't.

d) Not so bad, thanks.

🔲 **30**

Student A's dialogues

a)

A1: *What have you been up to lately?*

B1: *Oh, not much – the usual.*

b)

A2: *Long time no see.*

B2: *Yes, it must be over a year.*

c)

A3: *Alice sends her love.*

B3: *Thank you. Give her mine.*

d)

A4: *How do you do.*

B4: *How do you do.*

Student B's dialogues

a)

A5: *Keep in touch.*

B5: *I will.*

b)

A6: *Thank you for a lovely evening.*

B6: *You're welcome. You must come again soon.*

c)

A7: *Don't forget to phone me.*

B7: *I won't.*

d)

A8: *How are you?*

B8: *Not so bad, thanks.*

---

2 Students work individually to choose three exchanges and invent a context for them.

3 Groupwork. Students discuss their ideas for 2.

4   🔲 **31 SB p 151**

Students can do this individually or in pairs. Play the recording for them to check their answers.

---

1 better   2 been   3 having   4 for   5 be
6 regards   7 will   8 Give   9 must   10 Take
11 See   12 after   13 Bye   14 journey   15 you
16 already

🔲 **31**

The long goodbye

(A = Ann; B = Bob)

A: *I'd better be going.*

B: *It's been lovely to see you.*

A: *Thank you for having me.*

B: *Thanks for coming.*

A: *I'll be off then.*

B: *Give my regards to your family.*

A: *I will.*

B: *Give me a ring.*

A: *Okay. I really must be off now.*

B: *Take it easy.*

A: *See you.*

B: *Look after yourself.*

A: *Bye for now.*

B: *Safe journey.*

A: *Love you.*

B: *Missing you already.*

---

5 Pairwork. Students write down as many ways as they can. You could make this a competition to see which pair can come up with the most.

Test

Scoring: one point per correct answer unless otherwise indicated.

1 1 to take
  2 to warn
  3 making
  4 hearing
  5 to be
  6 living
  7 seeing
  8 to pick up
  9 playing
  10 living

2 (2 points per correct answer)
  1 used to
  2 'd
  3 'll
  4 didn't use to
  5 would
  6 will

3 (2 points per correct answer)
  1 will insist on kissing
  2 's always trying
  3 's forever talking about
  4 'll keep using
  5 'll insist on getting
  6 's always telling

4 1 scored
  2 players
  3 stadium
  4 won
  5 support
  6 lose

5 *Ritual* Test

Name: **Total:** _____ /40

1 Verb patterns *10 points*

Underline the correct form.

1   I'd like **to take / taking** this opportunity to congratulate Liz on her new job.

2   Helen tried **to warn / warning** them about it.

3   Will you stop **to make / making** so much noise!

4   I remember **to hear / hearing** this joke before.

5   I'd hate **to be / being** a doctor or a nurse.

6   John really likes **to live / living** in his new flat.

7   I remember **to see / seeing** a bright light in the sky.

8   We stopped **to pick up / picking up** a hitchhiker.

9   I loved **to play / playing** tennis when I was young.

10   Sandra hates **to live / living** in the country.

2 Past & present habits *12 points*

Complete the sentences using *will*, *would*, *used to* or *didn't use to*.

1   I _____ love going to the seaside as a child. Building sandcastles was great fun.

2   When I was younger I _____ often get into fights with my older brother. We hated each other then!

3   My sister hates getting up. She _____ always wait until the last minute before getting out of bed.

4   I _____ enjoy science subjects at school, because I wasn't very good at them.

5   My grandfather _____ always come round for dinner at our house on Sundays.

6   If there's a party, Tina _____ be there!

3 Annoying habits *12 points*

Complete the text with the expressions in the box.

> 'll keep using   will insist on kissing   's always telling
> 'll insist on getting   's forever talking about
> 's always trying

I dread my Aunt Rita's visits. She sweeps into the house wearing her designer outfits and bright red lipstick and then she (1) _____ me on both cheeks. She (2) _____ to tell me what I should be doing with my life. She (3) _____ what a model student she was and all the great things she did when she left school. Then she (4) _____ long words, thinking she's impressing me. When she leaves, she (5) _____ me to walk her to her car. And off she goes. The funny thing is, although she (6) _____ me what a great career she had, Dad said she's never actually done a day's work in her life.

4 Vocabulary – football *6 points*

Complete the sentences with appropriate words.

1   When the other team _____ their fourth goal, we knew it was all over.

2   How many _____ are injured this week?

3   There was a fantastic crowd. The _____ was completely full.

4   If their goalkeeper hadn't made such a fantastic save, we would have _____ the match.

5   I _____ Arsenal because they're my local team.

6   If we _____ another match it's going to be a very difficult season.

6 *Digital* Overview

The topic of this unit is modern technology and its effect on lives, particularly children's lives. The grammar focus is on verbs with stative and dynamic meanings and the use of the present perfect simple and continuous with such verbs.

Students start by completing an article about text messaging and using a key to write and transcribe their own text message conversations.

They then read an interview about computer use and use the questions to interview each other.

They practise differentiating between verbs with stative and dynamic meanings and look at the tense forms used with each.

Students discuss computer games and by listening to an interview with Lara Croft, the fictional heroine of the computer game, *Tomb Raider*, they find the answers to a quiz.

Students then practise the use of the present perfect simple and continuous with verbs with stative and dynamic meanings. They then read an article on how modern technology and changes in society have affected the way children play.

The unit ends with a writing exercise in which students present an argument for and against mobile phones.

Section	Aims	What the students are doing
Introduction page 52–53	*Reading skills*: reading for detail	Completing an article about text messaging and using a key to write and transcribe short text messages. Completing a text by matching questions to answers.
Close up pages 54–55	*Grammar*: verbs with stative and dynamic meanings	Differentiating between verbs with stative meanings and those with dynamic meanings. Learning about using appropriate tenses with these verbs.
Lara Croft page 56	*Conversation skills*: fluency work	Discussing favourite computer games.
	Listening skills: listening for detail	Listening to an interview with Lara Croft and completing a quiz about her. Writing and answering personal quizzes.
Close up pages 57–58	*Grammar*: present perfect simple and continuous	Practising the form and use of the present perfect with verbs with stative and dynamic meanings.
Child's play pages 59–61	*Reading skills*: scanning	Scanning an article to find what particular numbers refer to.
	Lexis: linkers	Using linking expressions to join sentences together.
	Discussion & listening skills: opinions	Giving opinions on the advantages and disadvantages of modern and old technologies. Listening to people talking on the same topic and comparing opinions.
	Writing skills: written arguments	Writing an argument about the advantages and disadvantages of mobile phones.

6 Digital *Teacher's notes*

Closed books. Find out how many students in your class own a mobile phone and how many of them bring them to class. Take advantage of their interest in mobile phones to get them to discuss the merits of each model and to say what functions each has. A student who is familiar with text messaging could demonstrate this facility to those who are not.

1 Ask students if they know what text messaging means (sending written messages on a mobile phone). Find out how many of them use mobile phones and whether they use text messaging – if so, how often.

Students work individually to complete the text. Check answers with the class.

1	less than the price of a call
2	nobody need know
3	are work-related
4	they'd like to know better
5	to write and phone more
6	too loud to talk
7	to your phone bill

2 Groupwork. Students discuss the question and report back to the class.

3 Pairwork. Students work together to rewrite the message in normal English.

Man:	Do you want to see me later for a drink
Woman:	What are you trying to say?
Man:	I love you. (Happiness)
Woman:	Oh, I see. (Surprise.)
Man:	Please call me.
Woman:	I'm with someone. (Sadness.)
Man:	What about your friend? I love her too. Is she with anyone?
Woman:	I hate you.

4 Students should be able to complete the key with little trouble.

Standard English	Text messaging
anyone	NE1
are you	RU
for	4
hate	H8
later	L8R

Standard English	Text messaging
love	LUV
oh I see	OIC
please call me	PCM
see	C
someone	SOME1
to, too	2
want to	WAN2
what	WOT
with	W/
you	U
your	YR

Emotion	Sign
happiness	;-)
sadness	:-(
surprise	:-0

5 Pairwork. Students write short text messages, exchange them with other pairs and then write the messages they receive out in full.

Reading (p 53)

1 Students can work in groups to write down all the words and expressions they associate with computers. Encourage them to organise the words into a spidergram, where possible. They then read the interview and add any new words. Tell them to ignore the missing questions at this stage.

2 Students match the questions to the numbered gaps in the interview. Check answers with the class.

a 7 b 4 c 8 d 3 e 6 f 9 g 10 h 5 i 12	
j 1 k 11 l 2	

3 Pairwork. Students take turns asking and answering five questions from the interview. They report any interesting information back to the class.

Close up (p 54)

Verbs: dynamic & stative meanings

1 Go through the extracts with the class and elicit answers to the questions.

Action: have a conversation, buy a juicer, say about the book

State: have a computer, be fantastic, like to see, not understand computers

have is used both for an action (in sentence *b*) and a state (in sentence *a*).

Refer students to the Language reference section on page 55 for more information about verbs with stative and dynamic meanings.

2 **32 SB p 54**

Play the recording as the students read the conversations. Then ask them to match the conversations with the pictures.

A 3   B 5   C 2   D 6   E 1   F 4

 32

(M = Man; W = Woman)

A

M: *Sorry, I didn't hear what you were ...*

W: *Of course you didn't hear. You weren't listening, were you? Sometimes I hate you.*

M: *Stop it. People are looking.*

B

M1: *I'm thinking of asking her to marry me.*

M2: *But you only met her last night!*

M1: *It seems like I've known her all my life.*

M2: *Yeah, right!*

C

W: *Look, over there. Is it a bird? Is it a plane?*

M: *No idea. I'm afraid I can't see a thing without my glasses.*

D

W: *You've only got one appointment this afternoon: you're seeing Mrs Lloyd at three.*

M: *Oh, not again. I hate talking to her.*

W: *Yes, but she likes listening to you.*

E

M: *Hey, what are you doing?*

W: *I'm tasting your soup. It smells great and it tastes delicious!*

M: *But it's not for you. So hands off!*

F

W: *We like each other.*

M: *And we want to be together.*

W: *That's true. But I don't think we love each other.*

M: *No, no. 'Course not.*

3 Pairwork. Students look at the verbs in bold and do the tasks. Check answers with the class.

a) Verbs with a stative meaning: (Dialogue A) hear, hate; (Dialogue B) seem, know; (Dialogue C) see; (Dialogue D) hate, like; (Dialogue E) taste, smell; (Dialogue F) like, want, think, love

B: Verbs with a dynamic meaning: (Dialogue A) listen, look; (Dialogue B) think; (Dialogue C) look; (Dialogue D) see; (Dialogue E) taste

b) Verbs with both stative and dynamic meanings: think, see, taste

c) Verbs with stative meanings cannot be used with the continuous form.

4 Students work individually to find the mistakes and correct the sentences. Check answers with the class before students turn five of the statements into questions and take turns asking a partner.

a) I have

d) I've known

e) I don't see

f) I want

h) I remembered

Lara Croft (p 56)

Books closed. Ask students what their favourite computer games are and why. Find out if there are any particular characters in these games that they like. Do they prefer human characters or doesn't it matter?

Listening (p 56)

1 If space allows, let students mingle around the classroom to find other students to talk to.

2 **33 SB p 151**

Focus students' attention on the illustration and the information about *Tomb Raider* in the margin. Then give them time to read the quiz and think about what Lara's answers might be. Finally, play the recording for students to listen to and tick the correct answers.

1 b   2 b   3 a, c, d, f   4 c   5 a   6 c   7 b

 33

Interview with Laura Croft

(I = Interviewer; LC = Lara Croft)

I: *Lara, you've become very famous. Has this changed your life?*

LC: *Not very much really. I mean, people recognise me if I go shopping or something, but I don't actually go out very much. The extra money is nice, but that's never been much of a problem for me anyway.*

I: *What do you think is the secret of your success?*

LC: *Well, some people say I've only been successful because of the way I look. But it's not true – I've succeeded because I've never let anything stand in my way.*

I: *But you do look exceptionally fit.*

LC: *I'm 1 metre 70 and I weigh 57.2 kilos, if that's what you mean. But I don't have time for people who are only interested in my figure. I need to keep in shape for my job, so I've been working out practically all my life.*

I: *How did you first get involved in these missions?*

LC: *By accident – literally. When I was at school in Switzerland, I took up extreme skiing and spent a holiday searching for challenging terrain. When I was flying home, the plane went down in the Himalayas. I was the only survivor, and it took me two weeks to reach civilisation. That was how I got a taste for adventure, and I've been going on missions ever since.*

I: *How long ago was that?*

LC: *Well, I've been doing this job since I was 21, and next Valentine's Day I'll be 32, so about eleven years.*

I: *How do your parents feel about your work?*

LC: *Well, they've been a bit frosty, since I started the job. They've also stopped my allowance because I tend to spend all my money on weapons.*

I: *Oh dear, how unreasonable. Lara, where do you live when you're not travelling?*

LC: *In a mansion in Surrey. I inherited it from my great-auntie about fifteen years ago and I love hunting in the woods.*

I: *Being a country girl, I suppose you like animals?*

LC: *Yes, they're delicious. I often bring my dinner in from the woods around my estate. I'm not a fussy eater though – I've tried all sorts of things in my time – smoked iguana, crispy tarantula and honeyed stick insects.*

I: *What do you do in your spare time?*

LC: *I spend any spare time at home cleaning my guns and preparing for the next adventure. Sometimes I get a film out – my favourite's 'Aguirre, the Wrath of God'. Truth is, I've never been very good at relaxing.*

I: *What sort of car do you drive?*

LC: *I've had my trusty old Land Rover for years, though I prefer my Norton Streetfighter motorbike for popping into the village.*

I: *Are you involved with anyone at the moment?*

LC: *No, I haven't been seeing anyone recently. My parents were trying to get me to marry the Earl of Farringdon. But although I liked him, I wasn't ready to commit. I hear he's still waiting for me.*

I: *Who is your ideal man?*

LC: *My hero is Brian Blessed.*

I: *Who?*

LC: *He's a Shakespearean actor – you'd recognise him if you saw him. But what I admire about him is his perseverance. He's tried to climb Everest three times and he's written a book about his trip to Mount Roraima in Venezuela. My dream is to ski down Everest with Brian Blessed strapped to my back.*

I: *Good heavens. You are an unusual person. Thank you Lara, and good luck with your next mission.*

3 Pairwork. Students work individually to write their quizzes, then exchange them with a partner. When they have completed them, they check their answers.

Optional activity

In pairs/small groups, students either choose a famous person they know a lot about or research a famous person (possibly using information from a website like www.biography.com if they have access to the Internet). They then prepare a quiz about him/her and try it out on another group.

Close up (p 57)

Present perfect simple & continuous

1 Read the sentences with the whole class and elicit answers to the questions.

a) Present perfect (simple and continuous)
b) Pair B and Pair C
c) Pair A
d) Pair B
e) Pair A
f) Pair C

2 Do this matching exercise with the whole class. If students have trouble with these forms, go through the Language reference section on page 58 with them.

a) 2 (Verb with dynamic meaning + the present perfect simple: the action is complete.)
b) 4 (Verb with stative meaning + the present perfect simple: the situation is incomplete or ongoing.)
c) 1 (Verb with dynamic meaning + the present perfect continuous: the action is incomplete or ongoing.)
d) 3 (Verb with stative meaning + the present perfect continuous: not usually used.)

3 Pairwork. Students choose the most appropriate forms and take turns asking the questions. Go round checking that they are asking the questions correctly.

> a) have you been saving
> b) Have you ever broken
> c) have you had
> d) Have you ever been
> e) have you been driving
> f) Have you ever missed
> g) Have you ever eaten
> h) have you taken
> i) have you known
> j) have you done

4 Students should work individually to complete the jokes, but allow them to compare answers with a partner.

5 ▭ **34 SB p 151**

Play the recording for students to check their answers. Ask if anyone can explain any of the jokes and if they found any of them funny.

> 1 've ever done
> 2 've been trying
> 3 's been
> 4 has just arrived
> 5 've received
> 6 's gone

> ▭ **34**
>
> **a)**
> *'This crossword is the most difficult I've ever done. I've been trying to think of one word for two weeks.'*
> *'How about "fortnight"?'*
>
> **b)**
> *'Waiter! This lobster only has one claw.'*
> *'I'm sorry, sir. He's been in a fight.'*
> *'Well, bring me the winner then!'*
>
> **c)**
> *'The invisible man has just arrived for his appointment, sir.'*
> *'Well, tell him I can't see him today.'*
>
> **d)**
> *I've received hundreds of replies to my ad for a husband. They all say the same thing: 'Take mine!'*
>
> **e)**
> *'My girlfriend's gone on holiday to the West Indies.'*
> *'Jamaica?'*
> *'No, she went because she wanted to.'*

Child's play (p 59)

Closed books. Tell students that they are going to read an article called *Has technology ruined childhood?* Ask them to predict the kind of things that will be discussed in the article.

Reading (p 59)

1 Pairwork. Students read the four statements and discuss them, deciding whether they agree or disagree.

2 Students read the article and find out what the numbers in the box refer to. If you want to give them practice in scanning for information, set this up as a race to see who can find the answers first. Then set aside some more time to allow them to read the article thoroughly.

> 1 in 7 children said that watching television would be their idea of a good day.
>
> Children from the age of 9 are now turning to their bedrooms as a place to socialise.
>
> 72% of children have a room they do not have to share with a sibling.
>
> 1% of children have an Internet connection in their bedroom.
>
> On average children devote 5 hours a day to screen media.
>
> 1 in 100 children can be classed as a real screen addict.
>
> 57% of children say they still enjoy reading.
>
> 1 in 5 teenagers can still be classed as a book-lover.

3 Pairwork. Students complete the sentences individually and then discuss whether they agree with them or not with a partner.

> a) devote
> b) losing
> c) classed
> d) draw
> e) shut
> f) kill

Linkers (p 60)

1 Students use sentences 1–7 to add to the summarising sentences a–g. Check answers with the class.

> a 2   b 4   c 6   d 3   e 1   f 7   g 5

2 Focus attention on the words in bold in sentences 1–7. Go through the headings in the table with the class and ask them to say under which heading each linker should go.

> *adding more information:* also

> *connecting contrasting ideas:* even so, on the other hand, yet, nevertheless
>
> *showing cause and effect:* as a result, consequently

3 Students go through the article on page 59 looking for more linkers and add them to the table. If you like, you could write the table on the board and get the students to call out linkers as they find them and tell you which section to write them in.

> *adding more information:* in fact, moreover
>
> *connecting contrasting ideas:* but, however, although
>
> *showing cause and effect:* because of this

4 Students could do this exercise individually or in pairs. Check answers with the class. There is more than one answer for each of them, so ask several students to say what linker they used.

> a)   A businessman in Swansea thought a bug had struck when his computer exploded. **But / However**, he discovered ...
>
> b)   An 80-year-old woman bought a Beatles single in the early sixties. **But / Yet / However**, she's never owned a record player. **As a result / Consequently / Because of this**, she hasn't heard it yet.
>
> c)   Air traffic control at Manchester Airport are worried that Furby toys may interfere with navigation equipment. **As a result / Consequently / Because of this** the toys have been banned ...
>
> d)   Thieves stole a stereo system and some tapes from a car in Rochester, Kent. **But / However**, they left ...
>
> e)   Mobile phones have been interfering with music played on the jukebox in a pub in Oxford. **As a result / Consequently / Because of this**, the offending gadgets have been banned.

Discussion & listening (p 61)

1 Groupwork. Students discuss the advantages and disadvantages of each item in the five pairs. Direct their attention to the Language toolbox for useful expressions for giving opinions. Go round offering help with vocabulary where necessary, but don't conduct class feedback at this stage.

2 📼 **35 SB p 151**
Play the recording. Students listen and see if any of the speakers express similar opinions to theirs. Encourage groups to tell the rest of the class which opinions they had in common with the speakers and where they differed.

📼 **35**

1

I love e-mail for speed and convenience, but I tend to write letters for pleasure. I love getting letters too. Hearing a letter drop through the letter box is much more exciting than getting an e-mail, even though it's usually a bill in my case.

2

I have mixed feelings about the Internet. Although I find it incredibly useful, I get fed up with it after about half an hour. There's a limit to how long I like to sit in front of a screen, whereas I can spend hours looking at books in the library.

3

Well, although I enjoy watching television, I actually think computer games are better because they're interactive.

4

It depends on what it is. I've booked flights online, and I've bought books and I'd probably buy boring stuff like washing powder and toilet rolls online. But I find shopping quite a social thing – I like to go round the shops with my friends, so I'd miss that if I did all my shopping on the Internet.

5

I think you can learn a lot from watching the right programmes on television, and it's a great way to relax as well. But I get far more out of reading a really good book.

Writing (p 61)

1 Give students plenty of time to think of ideas and to write their two lists.

2 Pairwork. Students compare their lists and choose three points in favour and three points against mobile phones. They then think about the consequences of each point.

3 Students write their arguments. Encourage them to plan their work using the outline given, and draw their attention to the Language toolbox which gives useful expressions for writing a discursive essay.

Test

1 1 S

2 D

3 D

4 S

5 D

6 D

7 S

8 S

2 (2 points per correct answer)

1 He's been surfing the Internet for two hours.

2 I've been waiting for Tom for an hour.

3 She's been staying with her aunt since Saturday.

4 How long has John been studying music?

3 (2 points per correct answer)

1 Have you seen

2 've been waiting

3 've been putting

4 have you saved

5 haven't counted

6 've heard

7 's been doing

4 (2 points per correct answer)

1 consequently / as a result

2 As a result / Consequently

3 also

4 On the other hand

5 Yet

Name: Total: _____ /40

---

1 Stative & dynamic verbs *8 points*

Mark the verbs in bold *S* (for stative) or *D* (for dynamic).

1   Jeff **knows** how to design websites.

2   I **see** my sister every weekend.

3   She **has** a shower every morning.

4   I really can't **see** why you won't help me.

5   Tara is **thinking** of going to college.

6   They **walk** to school everyday unless it's raining.

7   She doesn't **remember** meeting him before.

8   I **think** mobiles with Internet access are fantastic.

2 Present perfect continuous *8 points*

Write present prefect continuous sentences.

1   Joe's surfing the Internet. He started two hours ago.

He _____

_____

2   I'm waiting for Tom. I started waiting an hour ago.

I _____

_____

3   She's staying with her aunt. She arrived last Saturday.

She _____

_____

4   John studies music.

How long _____

_____ ?

3 Present perfect simple & continuous *14 points*

Complete the dialogue with the present perfect simple or continuous.

A: (1) _____ (you see) those new robot pets they make in Japan?

B: Yeah, they're great. I've always said the kids couldn't have a pet, so they (2) _____ (wait) for something like this for ages.

A: Aren't they really expensive?

B: No problem. I (3) _____ (put) my loose change in a jar ever since January.

A: How much (4) _____ (you save)?

B: I'm not sure. I (5) _____ (not count) it recently, but I must have over £50.

A: Oops. I (6) _____ (hear) they cost more than that. Closer to £500, I'd reckon.

B: Well, my company (7) _____ (do) a lot of work with Sony recently. Perhaps I can get a discount!

4 Linkers *10 points*

Complete the text with a suitable expression.

> yet   as a result   consequently   also
> on the other hand

It is said that modern children are obsessed with technology and (1) _____ spend all their time in front of computer screens. (2) _____ they are getting little or no exercise. TVs, music centres and personal stereos (3) _____ feature strongly in the typical teenager's life.

(4) _____ in a recent survey, the most popular activity for boys was playing football. Clearly, many have access to modern technology.

(5) _____ , given the choice, they still prefer to spend their time in active physical pursuits, doing very much what their fathers did at the same age.

---

7 *Review 1* *Teacher's notes*

In the dog house (p 62)

Present & past tenses

1 recently bought
2 inherited
3 signed
4 has never been
5 've been working / 've worked
6 said
7 explained
8 had earlier rejected
9 has
10 owns
11 has already made
12 tours
13 takes
14 is currently thinking
15 says
16 hear

Interview with Madonna (p 62)

Indirect questions

1
a) 'I'd like to know how your children have changed your life.'
b) 'Do you think you will have any more children?'
c) 'Could you tell me if you enjoy scheming up new images all the time?'
d) 'Do you think you will ever have plastic surgery?'
e) 'Would you say that you have traded love for fame?'
f) 'Do you mind telling me what your star sign is?'
g) 'I was wondering why you stopped going to the gym.'

2
a3 b4 c6 d2 e7 f1 g5

3 Pairwork. Students make up their own indirect personal questions and take turns asking a partner.

Four in a row (p 63)

Verbs & adjectives + prepositions

Students follow the rules and play the game.

Salad surprise! (p 63)

Articles

1 a
2 –
3 the
4 –
5 a
6 A
7 a
8 the
9 –
10 The
11 A
12 the
13 the
14 –
15 the
16 the
17 The
18 a
19 the
20 – / a

Five years in space (p 64)

Unreal conditionals

1 Students decide which item they would take and why.

2 Whole class mingling. Students move around the class finding out what other people chose.

Agony aunt (p 64)

Advice & recommendations

1 Students work individually to complete one of the letters.

2 Pairwork. Students exchange letters and give advice.

3 Students exchange letters with more students and decide who gave them the best advice.

Wise words (p 65)

Phrasal verbs

1

a 3	b 5	c 1	d 6	e 4	f 8	g 2	h 7

2

a) The trouble with children is you can't *give them back*.

b) Never *put off* until tomorrow what you can do the day after.

c) I *let* my friends *down*, I *let* my country *down*.

d) I haven't asked you to make me young again. All I want is to *go on* getting older.

e) To make a mistake is human, but to really *mess things up* you need a computer.

f) America is the only country where you buy a lifetime supply of aspirin for $1 and *use it up* in a week.

g) If you *give up* smoking, drinking and loving, you don't actually live any longer, it just seems longer.

h) The only way to *get rid of* temptation is to *give in* to it.

Mad millionaires (p 65)

Past habits

1

a) used to be; used to stay / would stay

b) used to be

c) used to be; didn't not allow / wouldn't allow; used to ask / would ask

d) used to steal / would steal

e) used to be; used to race / would race

f) used to walk / would walk; used to love / would love

2 Pairwork. Students discuss which of the millionaires had the craziest habit.

Maze (p 66)

Verbs + infinitive and/or *-ing* form

1 Pairwork. Students follow the instructions and find their way through the maze.

(Sentences in the correct sequence.)

I aim *to be* a millionaire in the next three years. (↘)

I fancy *watching* a really scary horror film tonight. (↑)

I really don't mind *doing* the ironing. (↑)

I hope *to go* round the world before I die. (↘)

I've decided *to take up* hang gliding. (↘)

I always finish *eating* before everyone else. (↑)

I seem to be unable *to remember* people's names. (↘)

I've tried *to learn* Arabic, but it's just too difficult. (↘)

My boss makes me *stay* late every night. (→)

My parents wouldn't let me *wear* make up until I was eighteen. (→)

I insist on *travelling* first class. (↑)

I've considered *joining* the circus. (↑)

I never offer *to lend* people money. (↘)

I'll never forget *going* to my first disco. (↑)

I keep *losing* my car keys. (↑)

I've taught myself *to play* the nose flute. (↘)

I tend *to be* rather bad-tempered early in the morning. (↘)

Correct FINISH: B

2 Students adapt three sentences from the maze to make them true for themselves.

Cryptic conversations (p 67)

Verbs: dynamic & stative meanings

1

a) think

b) are you thinking

d) 'm seeing

c) Do you see

e) do you weigh

f) are you weighing

g) are you smelling

h) smell

i) 're having

j) don't have / haven't got

a 6	b 8	c 2	d 5	e 7	f 9	g 3	h 10	i 1	j 4

2 Pairwork. Students add to the conversations and act them out.

Thumb trouble (p 67)

Present perfect simple & continuous

1

a) She sucks her thumb.

b) No.

c) She's been having therapy for several years. She's tried putting mustard on her thumb. She's had hypnosis. She's taken up smoking a pipe. She's worn gloves (even in bed).

d) He suspects that it's Debbie who has been sucking her thumb.

2

1 's been sucking

2 Has she ever tried

3 's been trying

4 hasn't succeeded

5 has she used / has she been using

6 's been having / 's had

7 Has it helped

8 's improved

9 hasn't stopped

10 's tried

11 's tried

12 've had / 've been having

13 've taken up

14 've worn / 've been wearing

3 ⏵ **36 SB p 152**

Play the recording for students to check their answers.

⏵ **36**

(C = Chris; D = Debbie)

C: *I'm a bit worried about Ellie. She's nearly six and she still sucks her thumb!*

D: *Oh, I shouldn't worry too much about Ellie. I've got a friend who's been sucking her thumb for twenty-nine years!*

C: *You're kidding!*

D: *No, honestly. She only does it when she's really tired, but you can imagine how strange it looks on a grown woman.*

C: *Very strange. Has she ever tried to give up?*

D: *Of course. She's been trying to give up since somebody called her a baby when she was twelve. But she hasn't succeeded yet.*

C: *What methods has she used?*

D: *Well, for example, she's been having therapy for several years.*

C: *Has it helped?*

D: *Not really. Well, I think it's improved some aspects of her life, but she hasn't stopped sucking her thumb.*

C: *There must be something she can do.*

D: *I know, but she's tried everything. She's tried putting mustard on her thumb, but she just got used to the taste, and actually started liking it. Now she has mustard on everything! And apart from that, I've had hypnosis, I've taken up smoking a pipe, I've worn gloves, even in bed ...*

C: *So do you suck your thumb too?*

D: *No!*

C: *You said 'I'.*

D: *Ah – no – I meant my friend ... has ... um ...*

4 Students discuss the questions.

5 Pairwork. Students write conversations. Encourage them to act them out for the class.

Mid Course Test

Scoring: one point per correct answer unless otherwise indicated.

1 (2 points per correct answer)
1   Did you see
2   we got
3   she had gone
4   are you going
5   we haven't decided
6   We always seem
7   Have you ever been
8   Dan and I would like
9   Did you come
10 it was raining
11 we left / we were leaving
12 I hadn't brought
13 Have you seen
14 he's
15 He's making
16 was she driving
17 the accident happened

2
1   have
2   would
3   Did
4   Has
5   did
6   had
7   didn't
8   haven't
9   shall
10 Would

3
1   how much you earned.
2   why you stopped seeing Jim?
3   if you've had a nose job.
4   what she said to him?
5   you'd ever have a tattoo?

4
1   at
2   to
3   of
4   on
5   in
6   with
7   about
8   for

5
1   An
2   a
3   a
4   the
5   the
6   –
7   the
8   the
9   a
10 the
11 an
12 the

6 (2 points per correct answer)
1   joined a gym, I'd be healthier.
2   found £100, I wouldn't keep it.
3   had enough money, I'd travel round the world.
4   known she was in hospital, I'd have visited her.
5   wanted to, I wouldn't have done it.
6   seen the letter, I'd have never found out.

7
1   were, 'd
2   Whatever, don't
3   Have, thought
4   best, not
5   would, idea
6   need, be
7   could, try
8   shouldn't

8 (2 points per correct answer)
1   got rid of
2   messed up
3   letting … down
4   went on
5   put off
6   giving up

9
1   used to
2   wouldn't
3   'd
4   used to
5   would

10
1   borrow
2   joining
3   to take up
4   losing
5   going
6   to ride
7   laugh
8   to lend
9   to meet
10 asking

11 1 're having
2 Do you see
3 's depending
4 'm enjoying
5 haven't got
6 do you think

12 1 haven't seen
2 've been going
3 've been learning
4 Have you been taking
5 've been
6 has cost
7 've been using
8 've gone

13 1 with
2 Chew
3 warmed
4 for
5 headache
6 mind
7 better
8 eyes
9 support
10 take
11 By the time
12 geek
13 humiliated
14 trickle
15 opinion
16 running
17 foot
18 centre
19 rainy
20 into

7 *Mid Course* Test

Name: Total: _____ /150

1 Present & past tenses *34 points*
Put the verbs into the most appropriate form.

A: (1) _____ (you see) Angela at the party last week?

B: No, by the time (2) _____

(we get) there, (3) _____ (she go).

* * *

A: Where (4) _____ (you go) on holiday this year?

B: (5) _____ (we not decide) yet. How about you?

A: Probably Wales. (6) _____ (we always seem) to end up going there.

* * *

A: (7) _____ (you ever go) to Australia?

B: Not yet, but (8) _____ _____ (Dan and I like) to go there soon.

* * *

A: (9) _____ (you come) home in a taxi last night?

B: Yes, (10) _____ (it rain) when

(11) _____ (we leave) the cinema

and (12) _____ (I not bring) my umbrella.

* * *

A: (13) _____ (you see) Paul anywhere?

B: Yes, (14) _____ (he be) in the

kitchen. (15) _____ (he make) dinner.

* * *

A: How fast (16) _____ (she drive)

when (17) _____ (the accident happen)?

B: About forty miles an hour.

2 Auxiliary verbs, question tags & short answers
10 points
Complete the sentences.

1 We've never met before, _____ we?

2 'I'd love to visit Japan.' 'So _____ I.'

3 _____ she pass her exams last year?

4 _____ anybody ever sent you flowers?

5 'I never used to like opera.' 'Neither _____ I.'

6 By the time we arrived, the band _____ already started.

7 You hated that film, _____ you?

8 'Have they been shopping?' 'No, they _____ .'

9 Let's stay a while longer, _____ we?

10 _____ you have gone if he'd asked you?

3 Indirect Questions *5 points*
Complete the indirect questions.

1 How much do you earn?

I was wondering _____

_____

2 Why did you stop seeing Jim?

Do you mind telling me _____

_____

3 Have you had a nose job?

I'd like to know _____

_____

4 What did she say to him?

Could you tell me _____

_____

5 Would you ever have a tattoo?

Do you think _____

_____

Photocopiable

4 Verbs & adjectives + prepositions *8 points*

Complete the sentences with an appropriate preposition.

1 She's always been useless _____ maths.

2 We're looking forward _____ going on holiday.

3 The training session consisted _____ a quick talk.

4 He insisted _____ dragging us out for a drink.

5 Josy specialises _____ solving problems.

6 This software isn't compatible _____ my PC.

7 She's really serious _____ moving out.

8 He's in the news again! What is he famous _____ ?

5 Articles *12 points*

Complete the newspaper article using *a/an* and *the* where necessary.

(1) _____ 88-year-old grandmother was disqualified from

(2) _____ walking race after breaking into (3) _____ run

when she was overtaken. Gabby Craig, (4) _____ oldest

competitor in (5) _____ race, thought she had (6) _____

victory in her sight but was stunned when Margaret

Turner, 74, took (7) _____ lead at (8) _____ halfway mark.

Mrs Craig was so outraged, she broke into (9) _____ run

and marched past two warnings from race officials at

(10) _____ trackside. Mrs Craig refused journalists

(11) _____ interview after (12) _____ event.

6 Unreal conditionals *12 points*

Write conditional sentences.

1 join a gym – be healthier

If I _____

2 find £100 – not keep it

If I _____

3 have enough money – travel round the world

If I _____

4 know she was in hospital – visit her

If I'd _____

5 not want to – not do it

If I hadn't _____

6 not see the letter – never find out

If I hadn't _____

7 Advice & recommendations *8 points*

Complete the sentences.

1 If I w_____ you, I'_____ see a doctor.

2 W_____ you do, d_____ tell her.

3 H_____ you t_____ of taking up a sport?

4 It's b_____ n_____ to overdo it at first.

5 It w_____ be a good i_____ to ask for help.

6 You'll n_____ to b_____ better dressed to get into that night club.

7 You c_____ t_____ washing it in bleach to remove the chocolate stain.

8 He told me I s_____ worry so much.

8 Phrasal verbs *12 points*

Complete the sentences with the correct form of the phrasal verbs in the box.

get rid of   give up   go on   let down
mess up   put off

1 We _____ that boring bloke at the club by telling him Madonna was at the bar.

2 I really _____ my exam by forgetting to answer the second part of the last question.

3 Tim was really disappointed with me for _____ him _____ last week.

4 He had so much work to do, we _____ working till 2 a.m.

5 We were really _____ going to that restaurant after we heard the food was awful.

6 Dave said that _____ smoking was the hardest thing he'd ever done.

9 Past habits *5 points*

Complete the text with the correct form of *used to* and *would*.

Kate (1) _____ be a very nervous child. She

(2) _____ go to bed until she'd checked in the

wardrobe for monsters. And she (3) _____ never

switch off the lights at night. She (4) _____ think

the shadows were monsters waiting to get her! Nothing we

said (5) _____ change her mind.

10 Verbs + infinitive and/or *-ing* form *10 points*

Underline the correct form.

1 My brother never lets me **borrow / to borrow / borrowing** his car.

2 I've never considered **join / to join / joining** a dating agency.

3 We've decided **take up / to take up / taking up** a new hobby.

4 You keep **lose / to lose / losing** your purse!

5 She insisted on **go / to go / going** by taxi.

6 Dad taught me how **ride / to ride / riding** a horse.

7 My friends always make me **laugh / to laugh / laughing**.

8 I'd like **lend / to lend / lending** you the money but I'm broke.

9 We arranged **meet / to meet / meeting** at the club.

10 She suggested **ask / to ask / asking** him to come with us to share the driving.

11 Dynamic & stative verbs *6 points*

Complete the sentences with the present simple or present continuous form of the verbs.

1 We _____ (have) a quiet night in tonight.

2 _____ (you see) what I mean?

3 I can't just not go. He _____ (depend) on me to help him.

4 I _____ (enjoy) this book very much.

5 I _____ (not have) enough time to look at this.

6 What _____ (you think) should be done?

12 Present perfect simple & continuous *8 points*

Complete the sentences with the present perfect simple or present perfect continuous form of the verbs.

A: Hi, Chris! I (1) _____ (not see) you for ages. How are you?

B: Fine – really busy though. I (2) _____ (go) to a photography class for the past few months. We (3) _____ (learn) loads of new stuff.

A: (4) _____ (you take) better pictures since you started the class?

B: Actually yes. I (5) _____ (be) really pleased with a lot of them. But all this photography stuff (6) _____ (cost) me a fortune.

A: How's that?

B: Well, I (7) _____ (use) my camera so much I (8) _____ (go) through twenty films in three weeks. I'm broke!

13 Lexis *20 points*

Underline the correct word.

1 He's lazy at school but he gets away **with / from** it.

2 **Chew / Eat** things over before making a decision.

3 You look like death **warmed / heated** up.

4 He always goes **for / at** tall blonde women.

5 I've got a splitting **sore throat / headache**.

6 You look worried. What's on your **mind / head**?

7 I'd **better / best** be going.

8 I've been up to my **eyes / ears** with this project.

9 What football team do you **support / believe** in?

10 Often you have to **take / make** a risk to succeed.

11 **As soon as / By the time** you read this, I'll be gone.

12 Do you see yourself as a computer **juicer / geek**?

13 When she laughed, I felt so **humiliated / amused**.

14 At first there was only a **drift / trickle** of interest.

15 In my **mind / opinion**, it should be banned.

16 We're **running / wasting** out of time.

17 He's always putting his **foot / mouth** in it.

18 He loves being the **middle / centre** of attention.

19 We're keeping this money for a **rainy / stormy** day.

20 The police are looking **into / at** the problem.

8 Escape *Overview*

The topic of this unit is holidays and travel. The grammar focus is on reporting verbs.

Students read an extract from *Notes From A Big Country*, a book by Bill Bryson, describing a terrible day at the beach with his family. They tell their own anecdotes about family holidays.

Students then study the form and use of reporting verbs and read a text about a boy who funded his luxury holiday by selling his mother's car while she was in hospital.

They then talk about holiday romances and listen to two stories about them, one a disaster and one a success.

Students look at different types of postcards and match them with descriptions of people who send them.

Next they study adjective building with a text about a journey from hell with three small children. This is followed by a matching exercise with extracts from city guides.

Finally, students play a board game which involves talking for thirty seconds on a variety of holiday-related topics.

Section	Aims	What the students are doing
Introduction page 68–70	*Conversation skills*: fluency work	Talking about beach holidays.
	Reading skills: reading for gist; scanning	Reading a text about a day at the seaside. Scanning the text for vocabulary items.
	Conversation skills: fluency work	Anecdote: talking about family holidays.
Close up pages 70–72	*Grammar*: reporting verbs	Putting a text summary in order. Studying the form and use of reporting verbs.
	Reading skills: skimming	Skimming a text to find the answer to a question.
I'll never forget you pages 72–73	*Conversation skills*: fluency work	Talking about holiday romances.
	Listening skills: listening for detail	Listening to people talking about holiday romances.
Weather lovely, … pages 73–74	*Reading skills*: reading for gist	Reading descriptions of people and matching them to postcards.
Journey from hell page 75	*Lexis*: adjective building	Using prefixes and suffixes to build adjectives. Completing a text about a bad journey using adjectives.
Insider's guide page 76	*Reading skills*: reading for detail	Matching cities with their descriptions.
The Travel Talk Game page 77	*Conversation skills*: fluency work	Playing a board game involving talking about different subjects for thirty seconds.

8 Escape *Teacher's notes*

Closed books. Ask students where they would love to be right now (instead of sitting in class). Ask them to provide reasons for their choices.

Open books. Divide the class into small groups and ask the groups to discuss the three questions about being on the beach. Ask one person in each group to feed back their group's answers to the rest of the class.

Reading (p 68)

1 Pairwork. Students list all the things they can think of that might spoil a day at the seaside. Allow pairs to compare notes with other pairs before getting feedback from the whole class. Find out if these things have ever happened to any of the students and encourage them to tell the story to the others.

2 Give students plenty of time to read the article. Ask them if Bill Bryson mentions any of the things they suggested in 1.

3 Students work individually to decide if the statements are true or false and then compare notes with a partner.

> a)
> 1 False   2 True   3 False
> b)
> 1 True   2 False   3 True
> c)
> 1 True   2 False   3 True

Optional activity

Students describe what they can see in the photograph on pages 68 and 69. They say whether or not they would enjoy this type of holiday.

Lexis (p 70)

Pairwork. Students complete the questions with the words and expressions in the box. Ensure they realise that they may need to make some changes to the words and expressions to make them fit. Students then ask and answer the questions.

> a)   tar
> b)   dermatologist
> c)   had a paddle
> d)   inflatable dinghy
> e)   nipped
> f)   put his/her foot down
> g)   slap
> h)   has a nap

Anecdote (p 70)

(See the Introduction on page 4 for more ideas on how to set up, monitor and repeat 'anecdotes'.)

Pairwork. Give students plenty of time to decide what they are going to talk about and to read the questions. They then take turns to tell their story to their partner.

Close up (p 70)

Reporting verbs

1 Whole class. Go round the class, student by student, establishing the correct order for the lines in the summary.

> 1 b   2 f   3 e   4 c   5 j   6 d   7 g   8 a   9 i
> 10 h

2 Elicit example sentences from the students which demonstrate the difference between *tell* and *say* before they categorise the highlighted verbs from 1. If students are unclear about reporting verbs, refer them to the Language reference section on page 72 for more information.

> List A: ... reassured me that ..., ... inform me that ...,
>   ... persuade me to ...
> List B: ... mention that ... , ... announce that ..., ...
>   insisted on ... , ... explained that ..., ...
>   suggested driving ...

3 Students look at the dictionary entries and add the verbs to their lists.

> List A: advise, assure, convince
> List B: admit, claim, complain, confirm, declare

Optional activity

Divide the class into two teams. As you call out verbs at random from the two lists, teams have to produce sentences. The first team to call out a correct sentence wins a point.

4 Closed books. Ask students to guess why a nineteen-year-old man was ordered by a court to pay his mother £68.70.

Students then read the newspaper report to find the answer.

He stole his mother's car and sold it without her knowledge. The court ordered him to pay his mother £68.70, the total amount she had spent on public transport since she had been without her car.

5 Students read the report again and choose the correct reporting verb in each case. Allow them to compare answers in pairs before checking with the class.

> 1 convinced   2 told   3 explained   4 claimed
> 5 assured   6 admitted   7 confirmed

6 Pairwork. Go through the instructions and the example with the class to ensure students know what they have to do. They then work in pairs to complete the exercise.

> 1 explained to people ...   2 announced to her ...
> 3 informed her ...   4 reassured her ...
> 5 declared to her ...   6 told reporters ...
> 7 assured them ...

7 Pairwork. Students discuss whether Christopher's punishment was appropriate. If they don't think it was, ask them to say what punishment they think would be right in these circumstances. When pairs have made their decisions, encourage a class discussion.

I'll never forget you (p 72)

Closed books. Write the words *holiday romance* on the board and ask students what they think they mean. Then make two lists on the board for the good and bad points of holiday romances and ask students to suggest ideas to put in each list.

Listening

1 Whole class. Elicit answers to the questions from the class. Encourage anyone who has had a holiday romance and is prepared to talk about it to give details to the class. However, be sensitive as students may find this embarrassing.

2 **37 SB p 152**
Go through the questions with the class and then play the recording. Students listen and find the answers. Encourage discussion of the students' answers to the final question and find out how many people sympathise with Angela, Brad or neither of them.

> a)   She was travelling in Australia.
> b)   They suspected that Brad had plans to work and hadn't just come on holiday.
> c)   She realised that the relationship was over.

 37

(T = Tony; A = Angela)

T: *Have you ever had a holiday romance, Angela?*

A: *I have actually. When I was twenty-six I went travelling to Australia. I went to Sydney – and while I was there I fell head over heels ...*

T: *No!*

A: *No, honestly, I really did. His name was Brad.*

T: *Brad?!!!*

A: *Yes, I know. Come to think of it, he did look a bit like Brad Pitt. Anyway, we met through a mutual friend, and to begin with I just worshipped him from afar – but then our mutual friend stepped in and arranged our first date. And that was it – the beginning of a beautiful relationship.*

T: *Ahh!*

A: *And actually, it's true – it was bliss. I was unbelievably happy. In fact, I really thought I'd met my soulmate – the person I would ... and could ... spend a lifetime with. Do you know what I mean? Anything ordinary we did felt extraordinary because we were together.*

T: *Yeah – I know what you mean.*

A: *I really did love him then ... in spite of what happened later.*

T: *Oh dear – what happened?*

A: *Well, eventually I returned to London. We spent six months on the phone. We swapped love letters, and parcels. He was the one who had never travelled, who didn't like his job, so it made sense that he should come here. Finally, the great day came, and I sat in Arrivals for ages, wondering what was holding him up. Meanwhile, he was being held by Customs because immigration officers suspected that he had plans to work and hadn't just come here on holiday.*

T: *Oh no!*

A: *Anyway, I finally got to see him, but I realised almost immediately that for me at least, it was over.*

T: *Oh no, why?*

A: *Well, basically, it wasn't the best of beginnings, was it?*

T: *No, I suppose not.*

A: *And to be honest, I don't think our relationship was strong enough for real-life problems.*

T: *So what happened to him?*

A: *Well, in the end he was deported back to Australia, and that was the last I heard of him.*

3 Play the recording again. Students listen and complete the gaps. Give them a few minutes to read their answers and compare with a partner before playing it again.

> a) Australia   b) Pitt   c) friend   d) soulmate
> e) extraordinary   f) London   g) beginnings
> h) strong   i) deported

4 Students look back at the bold words and expressions in 3 and match them to the meanings.

> 1 i   2 e   3 a   4 b   5 d   6 c   7 f   8 h   9 g

5 Students complete the gaps in the conversation with the appropriate expressions from 3. Do not check answers at this stage.

6 ▭ **38 SB p 152**

Play the recording for students to check their answers.

> 1   Actually
> 2   come to think of it
> 3   Anyway
> 4   Do you know what I mean?
> 5   Basically
> 6   to be honest
> 7   eventually
> 8   In fact
> 9   in the end

> ▭ **38**
>
> (T = Tony; G = Gill)
>
> T: *You're not the type to have a holiday romance, are you, Gill?*
>
> G: *Actually, I am. In fact, I met my husband on holiday.*
>
> T: *No!*
>
> G: *Yes, it's true. I went on a camping holiday in Scandinavia with some university friends, and Ash came along at the last minute.*
>
> T: *Camping in Scandinavia? Not exactly tropical ...*
>
> G: *No, come to think of it, it was a bit cold at times. Anyway, as soon as I saw him I thought, 'Yes, this one's for me.' Do you know what I mean?*
>
> T: *Oh yes, I know what you mean.*
>
> G: *But then I found out he had a girlfriend back home.*
>
> T: *Oh no!*
>
> G: *Basically I had two weeks to impress him – so I used my best weapon: I put on my little black dress ...*

> T: *I thought you said it was cold ...*
>
> G: *Yes, it was, but, to be honest, I didn't notice the temperature. And anyway, it was worth it because it worked – he resisted for a few days, which felt like years! But eventually he surrendered, and we spent the rest of the holiday together. In fact, we were inseparable.*
>
> T: *What happened when you got home?*
>
> G: *It was a horrible time because we knew we wanted to be together, but we both had other relationships to sort out.*
>
> T: *That must have been difficult.*
>
> G: *It was, but it all worked out well in the end. I mean, it's our fifth wedding anniversary in June.*

7 Pairwork. Students practise the conversation aloud, taking turns to be Gill and Tony. Make sure they concentrate on getting the stress and intonation correct. Ask several confident pairs to perform the conversation for the class.

Weather lovely, ... (p 73)

Closed books. Write *Wish you were here* on the board and ask students where they would expect to read these words.

Ask students when they last received a postcard, who it was from and what it said. Ask them to say what kind of things they normally write on postcards.

Whole class. Focus students' attention on the five postcards and discuss the questions with the class.

Reading (p 74)

1 Give students time to read the article thoroughly and to match the character types to the postcards. They can check the answers at the end of the article.

2 If you wish, you could do this as a whole-class activity with students raising their right hands if they think a statement is true and their left hands if they think it is false.

> a) False   b) True   c) True   d) True   e) True
> f) False   g) False   h) True   i) False

3 Pairwork. Students discuss the five character types and say if they know anyone who fits them.

Journey from hell (p 75)

Closed books. Ask students if they know what *it was the journey from hell* means (it was a journey on which everything went wrong and which the speaker did not enjoy at all). Ask them if they know any other expressions using *from hell*. Common ones are *the neighbours from hell*, and *the holiday from hell*. Invite them to describe what *the teacher from hell*, *the school from hell* or *the friend from hell* might be like.

Adjective building (p 75)

1 Students build adjectives with the affixes *well-* and *-conscious*. Check answers with the class. They then write sentences illustrating their meanings.

> well-read, well-known, well-meaning, well-dressed
> safety-conscious, self-conscious, health-conscious

2 Students make adjectives negative by adding prefixes. Allow them to find the negative adjectives in the article on page 74 before checking answers.

> incapable, illegible, impatient, indecisive,
> unadventurous, uninteresting, unusual, irresistible

3 Make sure students understand that the same prefix must be used with each of the words in each set.

> Set 1: im (immature, impolite, improbable)
> Set 2: il (illegal, illiterate, illogical)
> Set 3: ir (irreplaceable, irrelevant, irresponsible)

Optional exercise

Ask students if they know any more adjectives that are made negative by the prefixes *im-*, *il-* and *ir-*. (Possible answers: *impossible, immodest, illicit, illegitimate, irreconcilable, irrational, irregular, irrelevant*.)

4 Give students plenty of time to read the story and rewrite the adjectives. Check answers with the class.

> 1 relentless   2 disobedient   3 devilish
> 4 undivided   5 stressful   6 irresponsible
> 7 regardless   8 hellish   9 tearful   10 helpful

Optional activity

Pairwork. Students take turns to describe what happened on the worst journey they have ever had.

Insider's guide (p 76)

Closed books. Ask students where their favourite cities are and what they like about them. Ask them to say what aspects of the cities they would put in a guide for tourists.

1 Pairwork. Students discuss the questions. Make sure they understand the difference between the last two questions. *What are they known for?* means *What are they famous for?*

2 Students read the questionnaire and match the answers to the cities in 1. Make sure they understand that each answer is about a different city. When you check answers, ask students to say which clues helped them to decide.

> 1 Madrid   2 Amsterdam   3 Dublin
> 4 Buenos Aires   5 Prague   6 Sydney

3 Pairwork. Students take turns to ask and answer the questions about their favourite cities.

The Travel Talk Game (p 77)

You will need sufficient dice and counters for each group. Students follow the instructions and play the game.

Test

> Scoring: one point per correct answer unless otherwise indicated.
>
> **1** 1 suggested
>   2 explained
>   3 persuaded
>   4 reassured
>   5 complained
>   6 confirmed
>   7 admitted
>   8 accused
>
> **2** 1 convinced
>   2 advised
>   3 explained
>   4 admitted
>   5 told
>   6 assured
>   7 admitted
>   8 claimed
>
> **3** 1 nap
>   2 tar
>   3 slapped
>   4 dermatologist
>   5 paddle
>   6 dinghy
>   7 nipped
>   8 foot down
>
> **4** 1 indecisive
>   2 improbable
>   3 illegible
>   4 unusual
>   5 irreplaceable
>   6 unadventurous
>   7 illogical
>   8 incapable
>
> **5** 1 relentless
>   2 devilish
>   3 irresistible
>   4 undivided
>   5 regardless
>   6 irresponsible
>   7 stressful
>   8 disobedient

8 Escape Test

Name: **Total:** _____ /40

1 Reporting verbs *8 points*

Complete the sentences with the verbs in the box.

accused   admitted   confirmed   complained   explained
persuaded   reassured   suggested

1   Michael _____ going to see a film.

2   Dan _____ how to send an e-mail.

3   I wasn't that keen but Ruth eventually
    _____ me to go with her.

4   We _____ him that it would all be fine.

5   Kay _____ that her food was cold.

6   The travel agent _____ that we were
    booked on the two o'clock flight.

7   Penny _____ that she had made a
    mistake.

8   She _____ him of telling a lie.

2 Reporting structures *8 points*

Underline the correct verb.

1   He **convinced / explained** me it was a good idea.

2   She **advised / suggested** him to come immediately.

3   They **explained / informed** to her that her car had
    been stolen.

4   I **admitted / promised** to her that I had done it.

5   We **told / announced** them that it was all over.

6   He **declared / assured** her that he had permission.

7   She **admitted / told** that she has been involved.

8   He **claimed / assured** that it was all a conspiracy.

3 Vocabulary – travel/holidays *8 points*

Complete the sentences with appropriate words.

1   I'm really tired after that big lunch. I think I'll go and
    have a short n_____ .

2   The last time I walked along that beach, I got
    t_____ from the boats all over my feet.

3   She was so offended by what he said that she
    s_____ his face.

4   Don't forget your sun screen. Remember what your
    d_____ told you last time you got badly
    burnt.

5   The sea looks gorgeous. I'm going for a
    p_____ .

6   Let's pump up the inflatable d_____ !

7   'Why is that little boy crying?' 'Because that dog has
    just n_____ him on the leg.'

8   My mother put her f_____ d_____
    and refused to let the children go swimming in the sea
    on their own.

4 Vocabulary – adjectives *8 points*

Make these adjectives negative with the prefixes *un, in, ir,
im* or *il*.

1	_____decisive	5	_____replaceable
2	_____probable	6	_____adventurous
3	_____legible	7	_____logical
4	_____usual	8	_____capable

5 Vocabulary – adjectives *8 points*

Make adjectives with the words by adding: the prefixes
un, ir, dis; or the suffixes *less, ful, ish*.

1   relent   _____

2   devil   _____

3   resistible   _____

4   divided   _____

5   regard   _____

6   responsible   _____

7   stress   _____

8   obedient   _____

Photocopiable

9 *Attraction* Overview

The topic of this unit is what makes one person attractive to another. The grammar focus is on passive report structures, *have/get something done* and unreal conditional clauses without *if*.

Students look at the results of a survey into perfect male and female faces and discuss whether they agree with the survey's findings. They then read and comment on a report describing research into the nature of beauty. The first listening activity is a radio discussion about cosmetic surgery. Students listen and match the points made with the speakers.

Work on passive report structures comes next, and then a further text on cosmetic surgery is used to practise *have/get something done*. Students discuss where the best place in their town is to get various things done.

Students read a report on speed dating and discuss whether they would consider trying it. They then examine the report for adjectives with positive and negative connotations.

Students listen to part of a *Blind Date* television show and predict which woman the man will choose. They write their own *Blind Date* questions and answers.

Finally they complete the lyrics of *Never Ever* by All Saints and write a conversation between the people in the song.

Section	Aims	What the students are doing
The perfect face page 78–80	*Conversation skills*: fluency work	Talking about perfect male and female faces.
	Lexis: words describing facial appearance	Matching expressions to describe parts of the face.
	Reading skills: scanning for information	Scanning a text to find if statements are true or false.
		Predicting whether people are likely to support or oppose cosmetic surgery.
	Listening skills: predicting	Listening to people's opinions on cosmetic surgery and matching statements to people.
Close up pages 80–82	*Grammar*: passive report structures; *have/get something done*	Rearranging sentences using passive report structures.
		Determining a rule for the use of *have/get something done*.
		Completing a text on cosmetic surgery.
Speed dating pages 82–84	*Reading skills*: scanning	Scanning a text for information to complete a table.
	Lexis: adjectives; word building; word stress	Scanning a text to see if adjectives have positive or negative meanings.
		Using compound adjectives to describe people.
		Examining changes in stress when adjectives are changed into nouns.
Blind Date pages 85–86	*Listening skills*: predicting; listening for detail	Listening to a game show and predicting which person the contestant will choose.
		Listening to the couple's account of their blind date and choosing the correct information.
Close up page 86	*Grammar*: unreal conditional clauses	Completing unreal conditional clauses without *if*.
Never Ever page 87	*Listening skills*: listening for detail	Listening to an All Saints song and filling in the missing words in the lyrics.
	Writing skills: conversation	Writing a conversation based on the song.

9 *Attraction* *Teacher's notes*

Closed books. Ask students what factors attract one person to another. Is it physical beauty, personality, wealth or something else? Is it true that opposites attract or are we attracted to people who are most like ourselves?

Elicit adjectives which students feel might be applied to the most handsome man and the most beautiful woman. Write the adjectives on the board. (They may be useful later in this section of the unit.)

The perfect face (p 78)

Groupwork. Students discuss the questions and report back to the class.

Read the introduction to the survey and look at the pictures with the whole class. Elicit opinions on whether they think the people are attractive and why.

Lexis (p 78)

1 Have a class vote on whether the faces represent the students' idea of the perfect male / female face.

2 Students match the words in the two lists. Make sure they understand that some of the items in column A can be matched with more than one item in column B. Check answers before doing the next part of the exercise. Students can write their descriptions of the perfect face. Ask a few confident students to read their descriptions to the class.

a) smooth skin
b) perfect teeth / perfect bone structure / perfect skin
c) sparkling teeth / sparkling eyes
d) full lips
e) a big nose / a big smile
f) a turned-up nose
g) good teeth / good bone structure / good skin / good cheekbones
h) high cheekbones
i) a square jaw
j) dimples in the cheeks

3 🔲 **39 SB p 152**
Students listen to five people answering the question. Ask students to say where their opinions matched or differed from their own.

🔲 **39**

1
A: *What do you think makes a face attractive?*
B: *Er, smooth skin, perfect teeth and sparkling eyes.*

2
A: *What do you think makes a face attractive?*
B: *Ooh, big eyes, full lips, oh, and a big smile.*
A: *Like Julia Roberts?*
B: *Exactly.*

3
A: *What do you think makes a face attractive?*
B: *It's probably easier to say what I don't like. On a man, I don't like a small nose – it doesn't have to be enormous, but a little turned-up nose on a man looks silly.*
A: *So you don't like Brad Pitt then?*
B: *Well, I like everything about him except his nose!*

4
A: *What do you think makes a face attractive?*
B: *Good bone structure. High cheekbones. For a woman, a small chin, and for a man, a square jaw.*

5
A: *What do you think makes a face attractive?*
B: *Oh, I love dimples.*
A: *Dimples?*
B: *Yeah. They're so cute.*
A: *Where do you like them?*
B: *Oooh!*
A: *No, I mean where on the face – you know, do you like a dimple in the chin?*
B: *Yeah, I quite like that, but I meant dimples in the cheeks when somebody smiles – oh, it's so cute.*

4 Groupwork. Students take turns to describe people they know using expressions from 2. Go round offering help and encouragement where necessary.

Reading (p 79)

1 Go through the statements with the whole class. Elicit the meaning of 'Beauty is in the eye of the beholder'.

(Everyone has their own idea of what constitutes beauty; whether people or things are beautiful or not depends on the attitude of the person looking at them.) Then give students time to read the article and decide if the statements are true or false.

a) False   b) False   c) True   d) False   e) True

2 Pairwork. Students discuss whether they personally agree or disagree with the statements in 1.

Listening (p 80)

1 Have a class discussion on whether students think it is a good or a bad thing that cosmetic (plastic) surgery is becoming more common. First establish that cosmetic surgery is done to improve the appearance. This can be because someone has had a terrible accident which has disfigured them or because someone simply wants to change their appearance in some way. Do any of the students know anyone who has had cosmetic surgery? In what circumstances do they think it is good or bad?

2 ▭ **40 SB p 153**
Students first look at the three photographs and read the captions. They then predict what each person's opinion on cosmetic surgery will be and give reasons for their predictions.

Play the recording for students to listen to and find out if they were right.

Jean Oldham: against
Rita Taylor: for
Michael Hirst: against

▭ **40**

(JO = Jean Oldham; RT = Rita Taylor;
MH = Michael Hirst)

JO: *Well, I work on a women's magazine, so you can imagine how many beautiful models I've met. But I'm also in daily contact with women who are not physically perfect, and I have to say that the most beautiful women I know are not the models – they are the intelligent, interesting women whose inner beauty shines out. I believe that true beauty comes from within, and no amount of cosmetic surgery can give you that.*

RT: *Yes, I agree with you, Jean, but not everybody has the confidence to let their inner beauty shine out. Plastic surgery can actually give people that confidence. I really don't think there's anything wrong with trying to improve on what nature has given you.*

MH: *Ah well, that's where I disagree with you, Rita. I think we should be grateful for what God has given us. The point is, it's selfish and indulgent of people to spend vast amounts of money on*

superficial improvements when there's so much poverty and sickness in the world.

RT: *Actually, it's not that expensive, you know, Michael. I mean having your nose done only costs the price of a vacation, and quite frankly, cosmetic surgery can do more for you than a vacation, because the benefits last longer.*

JO: *Well, I don't know about that. I agree with Michael. I think that we should accept ourselves as we are and refuse to be influenced by stereotypical ideas of beauty.*

RT: *I'm sorry, but I don't think you're being very honest, Jean. I read your magazine and I frequently read articles encouraging women to have their hair dyed or highlighted. And do you ever go to the dentist, Michael? What do you think about people who have their teeth straightened? If you ask me, it's no different from having cosmetic surgery.*

MH: *Hang on, Rita. I think we have to make the distinction here between having something done for health reasons and having some part of your body changed simply because you don't like it ...*

JO: *Or because you want to stay young. Of course it's good to keep healthy, do sport, use sunscreen, that kind of thing, but I love to see life experience showing on people's faces. These aging film-stars who've had so much cosmetic surgery ... they all look the same.*

RT: *It's easy for you to say that, Jean, because you're lucky enough to be a good-looking woman. But if you're honest, I'm sure you will admit that your looks had something to do with you getting the job you have.*

JO: *Rita, are you suggesting ...*

MH: *Oh, this is rubbish, Rita. You're talking about a very different world from the one I know.*

RT: *Look, you two may not agree with it, but it's a fact of life. People who feel good about the way they look are more likely to do well in their career – good looks open doors.*

3 Pairwork. Students read the points and try to remember who made each one. They can write the initials of the person next to each statement. Then play the recording again for them to check their answers.

a) Jean Oldham   b) Rita Taylor   c) Rita Taylor
d) Michael Hirst   e) Michael Hirst   f) Rita Taylor
g) Jean Oldham   h) Rita Taylor   i) Jean Oldham
j) Rita Taylor

4 Pairwork. Students discuss which of the points they agree with. Go round offering help with vocabulary where necessary.

Close up (p 80)

Passive report structures

1 Read the extracts with the class and elicit answers to the questions.

> a) people in general
>
> b) It's usually good to use the passive when you are talking about what people in general feel or believe.

2 Students rearrange the words to make the beginnings of sentences. Check answers with the class.

> a) Our capital city is reckoned ...
>
> b) English food is said ...
>
> c) It is wrongly believed that all blondes ...
>
> d) It has been claimed that eating carrots ...
>
> e) Princess Diana was thought ...
>
> f) It is often suggested that men ...
>
> g) Politicians are not regarded ...
>
> h) It is sometimes assumed that unmarried women ...

3 Students match the sentence beginnings they formed in 2 to the sentence endings.

> a 4   b 6   c 8   d 5   e 3   f 7   g 1   h 2

Have/Get something done (p 81)

1 Focus students' attention on the cartoon. Ask them to explain what the joke is. (The woman has gone to a lot of trouble to get ready for a party, then finds that the party is tomorrow so she'll have to do it all again.) Then go through the questions and elicit answers.

> a) Helen did.
>
> b) Someone else did.
>
> c) In sentence 2: *Helen got her hair done before her friend's birthday party.*

2 Students complete the rule by choosing the correct ending. Direct them to the Language reference section on page 82 if they have difficulty. Ask them to come up with example sentences about things that they have done.

> b) You can use the structure *have something done* when someone does something for you.

3 Students complete the text. Check answers and then ask students whether they like Cindy's appearance as shown in the photograph.

> 1 had   2 Having   3 have   4 had   5 had
> 6 had   7 having   8 had   9 had

4 Groupwork. Students discuss the question and report back to the class. Try to find out how they would define 'better'. Can they see any disadvantages to attracting attention just because you are pretty?

5 Students reorder the sentences and then rewrite them so that they are true for themselves.

> a) I have my letters typed by my secretary.
>
> b) I wash my car on Sundays.
>
> c) I get my hair cut every six weeks.
>
> d) I clean my house at the weekend.
>
> e) I have my nails manicured regularly.

6 Groupwork. Students should be able to discuss these questions whether they are all from the same town or not. Direct them to base their discussion on the town they are in now.

Speed dating (p 82)

Closed books. Groupwork. Ask students to make a list of all the ways they think people use to find a boyfriend or girlfriend. Then ask them to decide which ways they think are likely to be the most successful and to number them in order. Groups then compare results.

Reading (p 82)

1 Groupwork. Students discuss the questions. You may need to explain *turn you off somebody* (make you lose interest in somebody), but do not explain *speed dating* and discourage students from looking at the material on the next page; allow them instead to predict what it might mean.

2 Pairwork. Students read the article about speed dating and complete the table. Then they answer the questions.

	Best date	Worst date		Best date	Worst date
Craig	Claire	Erica	Karen	Craig	Tony
Kevin	Sindy	Lara	Lara	Adam	Jim
Adam	Karen	Erica	Sindy	Tony	Adam
Jim	Sindy	Claire	Erica	Adam	Kevin
Tony	Sindy	Lara	Claire	Adam	Tony

> a) The most popular: Adam;
>   the least popular: Tony
>
> b) The most popular: Sindy;
>   the least popular: Erica and Lara
>
> c) Kevin and Tony.
>
> d) Tony and Sindy

3 Pairwork. Students discuss in pairs whether they would ever try speed dating. Encourage them to give reasons for their decisions.

Lexis (p 84)

1 Students make their decision before finding the words in the article. They then look back and check.

> a) Negative   b) Positive (though sometimes negative)
> c) Positive   d) Positive   e) Negative
> f) Positive   g) Positive   h) Positive
> i) Negative (though sometimes positive)
> j) Positive   k) Positive

2 Students work individually to replace the words in bold, but allow them to compare with a partner before you check answers.

> a) sensitive; trustworthy   b) sensible   c) laid-back
> d) stand-offish   e) straight, open-minded
> f) mature   g) enigmatic   h) down-to-earth
> i) self-centred

3 Pairwork. Ensure students understand *identify with*. (Do they feel these sentences are applicable to themselves?)

Word building (p 84)

1 Elicit some more examples of adjectives that can be turned into nouns by adding *ity* and *ness*. Students then transform the adjectives in the box.

> flexible – flexibility
>
> lively – liveliness
>
> friendly – friendliness
>
> compatible – compatibility
>
> sad – sadness
>
> generous – generosity
>
> weak – weakness
>
> mature – maturity
>
> sexy – sexiness

2 Elicit an example of a compound adjective. Students then join words from the boxes. Ask for example sentences illustrating the meaning of the compound adjectives.

> b) two-faced   c) self-assured   d) big-headed
> e) warm-hearted   f) stuck-up   g) quick-witted
> h) easy-going

3 Pairwork. Students take turns to describe family members or friends using the words in 1 and 2. The listening partner then says whether they would like to meet them or not.

Word stress (p 84)

1 📼 **41 SB p 84**
Students mark the stress on the words before you play the recording. They then listen and check their answers.

> <u>sen</u>sitive   <u>hap</u>py   <u>flex</u>ible   <u>live</u>ly   <u>friend</u>ly
> com<u>pat</u>ible   <u>sad</u>   <u>gen</u>erous   <u>weak</u>   ma<u>ture</u>   <u>sex</u>y

2 📼 **42 SB p 84**
Students mark the stress on the words before you play the recording. They then listen and check their answers.

> sensi<u>tiv</u>ity   <u>happi</u>ness   flexi<u>bil</u>ity   <u>live</u>liness
> <u>friend</u>liness   compati<u>bil</u>ity   <u>sad</u>ness   gene<u>ros</u>ity
> <u>weak</u>ness   ma<u>tur</u>ity   <u>sex</u>iness

3 Ask students to say what the effect on the word stress is when you add the two suffixes.

> When you change an adjective into a noun by adding the suffix *ity*, the stress generally moves to the syllable before the suffix.
>
> When you change an adjective into a noun by adding *ness*, the stress doesn't change.

Blind Date (p 85)

Listening

Explain *blind date* (two people who have not met before go out together) and ask students if they have ever been on a blind date or if they know someone who has. Who set up the blind date? How did they recognise the person? Was it successful? What happened?

1 Read about the television programme *Blind Date* with the class. Elicit answers to the questions.

2 Whole class. Elicit students' responses to the photograph of James. Encourage them to speculate about what kind of person he is and what kind of person his ideal date would be.

3 Pairwork. Students read the three questions and discuss what their answers would be. You may need to explain the saying *The way to a man's heart is through his stomach* (a woman can attract a man if she is a good cook).

4 📼 **43 SB p 153**
Play the recording. Students listen to three women answering the questions and try to visualise them. (Point out that the women on the recording are *not* the women in the picture at the top of the page.) Then in pairs they discuss what they think the women look like.

43

(C = Cilla; J = James)

C: So what's your first question, James?

J: They say that the way to a man's heart is through his stomach, and I must say, I do like my food. If you were to cook me a meal, how would you impress me? ... And that question goes to Number 1.

No 1: Actually, I'm not a very good cook. But when you choose Number 1 tonight, the only tasty thing on your mind will be me.

J: Number 2?

No 2: Hello, James.

J: Hello.

No 2: My speciality is chocolate mousse – it's sweet, dark, delicious and bubbly – just like me.

J: Okay. And finally to Number 3.

No 3: Well, James, I'd make sure you ate plenty of spinach, 'cause like Popeye, you'll need all your strength to keep up with me!

C: And your second question, James?

J: I've got two pet frogs which my friends say are like me – a good set of legs, like a drink and come alive in the evening. Imagine you had a pet that reflected your personality, and what would it be? ... That question for Number 2.

No 2: Well, I'd have to be a koala bear – my enormous brown eyes make me irresistible, and you'll want to cuddle me all night.

J: ... and Number 3.

No 3: I don't want to frighten you, but I have earned the reputation for being a bit of a man-eater. So I'd have to describe myself as a man-eating tiger, because when I go after something, there is no escape.

J: Number 1.

No 1: It would have to be a fox, 'cos I'm sly, cunning and naturally foxy. So you're going to have to chase me if you want to catch me.

C: It's time for your last question, Chuck. I hope it's a good one.

J: I'm a very superstitious sort of person and I believe that wishes can come true. If one of your wishes were to come true, what would it be? And that goes to Number 3.

No 3: Well, James, I wish that Numbers 1 and 2 would disappear, so that you and I could start our date right now.

J: And Number 1, please.

No 1: I had my palm read by a gypsy recently, and she told me that I would meet a tall, dark, handsome stranger before my next birthday. Guess what – it's my birthday tomorrow.

J: And finally to Number 2.

No 2: James – I wish the screen between us was transparent – because if you could see me, you'd know that I was the only one for you.

5 Pairwork. Students discuss what they have heard and answer the questions. Encourage them to have a full discussion before they turn to page 137 to find out which one James picks.

6 44 SB p 153

Go through the questions with the class. Then play the recording. Students listen to find the answers.

a) Yes.

b) No.

44

(J = James; M = Melanie)

M: When the screen went back, I was expecting a tall, dark, handsome man. But what I saw was tall, dark and not very handsome.

J: I think Mel loved my eyebrows. I think she fell in love with them as soon as she saw them. Everybody else does.

M: I didn't fancy James, and it was probably partly because of his eyebrows. He's extremely proud of them, but I think they look like a couple of caterpillars.

J: During the date, I talked about myself, my character, my personality, my job, because I really wanted Melanie to get to know me. Melanie is actually quite serious and rather difficult to get to know. She wasn't very talkative and she didn't tell me much about herself. But I think she liked all my jokes.

M: During the date, James talked about himself non-stop, and it was quite clear that he wasn't interested in getting to know me at all. He's very talkative. In fact, I didn't get a chance to say anything really. He laughed a lot at his own jokes too. At first, I thought he was really funny, but then I got a bit tired of his jokes and I wanted to talk about more serious things – you know, get to know him a bit better.

J: Mel is a total flirt – she was all over me like a rash.

M: I'm an affectionate sort of person, but there was no kissing on the date. It would have been like kissing my brother.

J: I think Mel fancied me more than I fancied her – basically her body language gave it away. Although I think Mel is pretty, I think she should work out a bit more and maybe lose a few kilos.

> M: *During the date, James said that he would give me eight out of ten if I lost four or five kilos. At the time, I thought the only weight I needed to lose was the man sitting next to me.*
>
> J: *I really thought the date went well and I'm looking forward to seeing Melanie again. She says she's busy for the next three months, but I'll call her then and, hopefully, something will develop between us.*
>
> M: *James is not my type at all. He's big-headed, self-obsessed and immature. Frankly, I feel sorry for the woman who ends up with him.*

7 Play the recording again. Students tick the correct information. Check answers with the class.

> Melanie thought that James ...
> b) had eyebrows like caterpillars.
> c) wasn't interested in getting to know her.
>
> James thought that Melanie ...
> a) was a total flirt.
> b) fancied him a lot.

8 Groupwork. Students make up answers to the questions. Encourage them to imitate the style of the *Blind Date* answers. Groups then compare answers and pick the best ones.

Close up (p 86)

Unreal conditional clauses

1 Students complete the questions. Check answers.

> a) were; be   b) would   c) would   d) were
> e) would; were   f) would   g) were; would
> h) were; would

2 Point out that only the first sentence in 1 uses *if*. However, all of them use unreal conditional clauses. Students underline the expressions that can be used instead of *if*. Refer them to the Language reference section for more information.

> b) Just imagine   c) Supposing   d) Assuming
> f) Assuming   g) Supposing   h) Suppose

3 Pairwork. Students ask each other the questions in 1 and find out how similar their attitudes towards dating are.

Never Ever (p 87)

Song

1 ▭ **45 SB p 154**
Go through the information at the side about All Saints.

Students try to complete the song. When they have finished, play the recording for them to check their answers.

> 1 few   2 hurt   3 done   4 long   5 paid   6 give
> 7 keep   8 make   9 to   10 on   11 in   12 have
> 13 right   14 start   15 out   16 answers

▭ **45**

Never Ever by All Saints

A few questions that I need to know:
How you could ever hurt me so?
I need to know what I've done wrong,
And how long it's been going on.

Was it that I never paid enough attention?
Or did I not give enough affection?
Not only will your answers keep me sane,
But I'll know never to make the same mistake again.

You can tell me to my face,
Or even on the phone.
You can write it in a letter.
Either way I have to know.

Did I never treat you right?
Did I always start the fight?
Either way I'm going out of my mind.
All the answers to my questions I have to find.

2 Pairwork. Students discuss the questions.

> a) Very depressed.
> b) Her boyfriend/partner/husband.
> c) Her boyfriend/partner/husband has left her or has been having an affair with another woman.
> d) She wants him to explain what has happened.

3 ▭ **46 SB p 154**
Students use the words in the box to complete the lines and then compare with a partner. Play the recording for them to listen and check their answers.

> a) daze   b) mind   c) wrong   d) hole   e) right
> f) pain   g) feeling   h) know

▭ **46**

My head's spinning.
Boy, I'm in a daze.
I feel isolated.
Don't wanna communicate.

I take a shower.

I will scour.

I will roam.

Find peace of mind.

The happy mind,

I once owned, yeah.

Flexing vocabulary runs right through me.

The alphabet runs right from A to Zee.

Conversations, hesitations in my mind.

You got my conscience asking questions that I can't find.

I'm not crazy. I'm sure I ain't done nothin' wrong.

No, I'm just waiting, 'cos I heard that this feeling won't last that long.

Never ever have I ever felt so low.

When you gonna take me out of this black hole?

Never ever have I ever felt so sad.

The way I'm feeling, yeah, you got me feeling really bad.

Never ever have I had to find.

I've had to dig a way to find my own peace of mind.

I've never ever had my conscience to fight.

The way I'm feeling, yeah. It just don't feel right.

(Never ever have I ever felt so low ...)

I'll keep searching deep within my soul

For all the answers – don't wanna hurt no more.

I need peace, got to feel at ease.

Need to be free from pain,

Go insane.

My heart aches, yeah.

Sometimes vocabulary runs through my head.

The alphabet runs right from A to Zed.

Conversations, hesitations in my mind.

You got my conscience asking questions that I can't find.

I'm not crazy. I'm sure I ain't done nothing wrong.

Now I'm just waiting, 'cos I heard that this feeling won't last that long.

(Never ever have I ever felt so low ...)

You can tell me to my face.

You can tell me on the phone.

Ooh, you can write it in a letter, babe,

'Cos I really need to know.

4 Pairwork. Students imagine the man's side of the story and think about the questions. They then write a conversation between the man and the woman. Go round offering help where necessary. Pairs then act out their conversations in front of the class.

Test

Scoring: one point per correct answer unless otherwise indicated.

1 (2 points per correct answer)
1. It is said that
2. is often thought to be
3. was reckoned to be
4. are believed to
5. It was once believed that

2 (2 points per correct answer)
1. Have you had
2. Did you have
3. had it repaired
4. haven't had the washing machine
5. 'm having my eyes tested
6. do you have your teeth polished

3 1. were; would
2. were; could
3. could; would
4. had; be

4 (2 points per correct answer)
1. compatible
2. open-minded
3. self-centred
4. tolerant
5. conventional

5 1. <u>fl</u>exible
2. <u>g</u>enerous
3. sensit<u>iv</u>ity
4. ma<u>ture</u>
5. gene<u>ros</u>ity

9 Attraction Test

Name: _____   **Total:** _____ /40

---

1   Passive report structures *5 points*

Complete the sentences with the correct phrases.

> is often thought to be   It is said that   are believed to
> It was once believed that   was reckoned to be

1   _____
    men prefer women with blonde hair.

2   France _____
    the food capital of the world.

3   For years, John _____
    the best-looking boy at my school.

4   The robbers _____
    have escaped on a motorbike.

5   _____
    the world was flat.

2   *Have something done* *12 points*

Complete the dialogues using *have*.

1   A: _____ your hair cut?

    B: No, I've just washed it.

2   A: _____ your house painted
         last week?

    B: Yes. Do you like the colour?

3   A: Your car's fixed now, isn't it?

    B: Yes. I _____ (it repair)
         yesterday.

4   A: Can I wash these clothes?

    B: No, I _____
         (the washing machine fix) yet.

5   A: What are you doing this afternoon?

    B: I _____
         (my eyes test).

6   A: How often _____
         (your teeth polish)?

    B: Every six months.

3   Unreal conditionals *8 points*

Complete the questions with appropriate words.

1   Imagine you _____ meeting someone's
    parents for the first time, what _____ you wear?

2   Supposing I _____ to come to your class, what
    _____ you teach me that I don't already know?

3   Imagine you _____ change an imperfect
    feature, what _____ you change?

4   Supposing that someone told you that you _____
    a twin brother, how would you _____ feeling
    now?

4   Vocabulary – adjectives of character *10 points*

Complete the sentences with an appropriate adjective.

1   Kim and Dave aren't at all c_____ .
    They've got nothing in common.

2   I'm quite o_____ , but I still think
    there's too much violence in films these days.

3   Cath is very s_____ . She never stops to
    think about other people.

4   My parents were always very t_____
    when I was growing up. They let me do my own
    thing.

5   Don was a very c_____ child. He just
    wanted to be like his friends.

5   Pronunciation – word stress *5 points*

Mark the word stress on each of the words.

1   flexible

2   generous

3   sensitivity

4   mature

5   generosity

---

10 Genius Overview

The topic of this unit is genius – the special ability displayed in the work of architects, artists and inventors. The grammar focus is on modals of deduction and narrative tense structures.

Students read about the design and construction of the Guggenheim museum in Bilbao and the life and work of the Mexican artist, Frida Kahlo. They examine some of her paintings to find evidence of her troubled life.

Students look at some of the inventions of the last five hundred years and evaluate their importance. They then listen to an interview with Trevor Baylis, the inventor of the clockwork radio, and complete a text on his life story. Stories of other inventors are used to practise narrative tense structures.

Finally, the students play a general knowledge board game, using some questions which they have written themselves.

Section	Aims	What the students are doing
The genius of Guggenheim pages 88–89	*Reading skills*: scanning, reading for detail	Scanning a text to find the adjectives used to describe different things. Reading a text to find connections.
I know what I like! pages 90–91	*Conversation skills*: fluency work	Discussing art and paintings.
	Reading skills: reading for detail	Matching aspects of Frida Kahlo's life to elements in her paintings.
	Listening skills: listening for gist	Listening to people discussing paintings and comparing their interpretation to yours.
	Lexis: collocation	Studying collocations connected to health.
Close up pages 92–93	*Grammar*: modals of deduction; word linking	Practising using modals of deduction for speculation. Practising linking unstressed words.
Eureka pages 93–95	*Conversation skills*: fluency work	Discussing and evaluating inventions.
	Listening skills: listening for detail	Listening to an interview and putting questions in order.
	Lexis: word families	Completing a table of word families.
Close up pages 95–96	*Grammar*: narrative tense structures	Completing narrative texts with appropriate tense structures.
Trivia pursuit – Genius edition page 97	Game	Playing a general knowledge board game.

10 Genius *Teacher's notes*

Closed books. Write the word *genius* on the board and ask students what it means (exceptional mental or creative ability and someone who possesses such ability). Ask them for the names of some people that they consider to be geniuses and get them to say what these people have done to deserve the name genius.

The genius of the Guggenheim (p 88)

Reading

1 Ask students if anyone has ever been to Bilbao in northern Spain. Ask them to tell the class what they did there and what they saw.

Focus attention on the photograph of the Guggenheim Museum. Students choose words from the box to describe it.

2 Students read the article to find which words are used to describe the museum, the city and the area around the museum. Encourage them to do this by scanning the article. There will be an opportunity later for them to read it more carefully. Check answers with the class.

> a) The Guggenheim Museum: metallic, post-modern, space-age, shiny, important, contemporary
>
> b) The city of Bilbao: 19th century, tough, sprawling, eccentric
>
> c) The area around the museum: hideous, semi-derelict, run-down

3 Give students plenty of time to read the article thoroughly and to explain the connections.

> a) Thomas Krens discovered the site for the museum while he was out jogging.
>
> b) The museum is surrounded by run-down derelict buildings – urban sprawl.
>
> c) Bilbao faces out onto the Bay of Biscay.
>
> d) The Basque government commissioned designers for lots of new buildings as part of their redevelopment programme to help to improve the city's global reputation.
>
> e) The city council chose a wine-bottling warehouse as the site for the museum.
>
> f) Thomas Krens had the Pompidou Centre and the Sydney Opera House in his head as the kind of space he wanted for the Guggenheim Museum.
>
> g) Frank Gehry loved the city and didn't want to change anything about the waterfront site.

4 Encourage students to complete the sentences without looking back at the text. They can then use it to check their answers.

> a) green hills
>
> b) redevelopment programme
>
> c) subway
>
> d) overcrowded
>
> e) overlooking
>
> f) run-down
>
> g) dominates
>
> h) well worth

Anecdote (p 89)

(See the Introduction on page 4 for more ideas on how to set up, monitor and repeat 'anecdotes'.)

Pairwork. Give students plenty of time to decide what they are going to talk about and to read the questions. Remind them that the Language toolbox contains some useful language which they can use in their descriptions. They then take turns to tell a partner about the most impressive building or monument they have ever seen. Encourage the listening partner to ask appropriate questions at the end.

I know what I like! (p 90)

1 Groupwork. Students discuss the questions. Encourage them to use the words from the box.

2 Pairwork. Students describe the paintings and discuss the story behind each. Go round offering help and encouragement and draw students' attention to the useful language in the Language toolbox.

3 Pairwork. Students look at the paintings and try to memorize as many of the details as they can. They then turn to page 137 and try to answer the questions without turning back to this page.

> *Frida and Diego Rivera, 1931*
>
> a) She's wearing a green dress, a red shawl and a pair of green and red shoes.
>
> b) Two necklaces and a pair of earrings.
>
> c) A palette and four paint brushes.
>
> d) A bird.
>
> e) Green/blue.

Self-portrait with cropped hair, 1940

a) She's got eyebrows that meet in the middle, and her dark hair is cut short, off her face. She looks serious, not very happy, but calm.

b) A man's suit.

c) A pair of scissors.

d) Wood.

e) Two lines of a song (some words and music notes).

Roots, 1943

a) It's rocky and barren.

b) Her hand or her arm, and her elbow is resting on a pillow.

c) Loose.

d) Her torso (the top part of her body).

e) Green with red veins.

4 Whole class. Students read the text about Frida Kahlo and suggest which aspects of her life they can see depicted in the three paintings. This is a subjective exercise with no right or wrong answers, but encourage students to give reasons for what they say.

5 🔲 **47 SB p 154**
Play the recording for students to listen and see how far their interpretations match those of the speakers.

🔲 **47**
(A = Andy; B = Beth; C = Chris)

A: *So this is her husband – Diego Rivera. She can't have fallen in love with him for his looks, can she? Ha ha.*

B: *No, I reckon he must have been either very rich or very intelligent.*

C: *Actually, he was both highly intelligent and very rich. At first, Frida's father was against her marrying Diego because he was a communist, but he finally agreed to it because he couldn't pay his daughter's medical expenses any more. Frida must have spent a fortune on doctors and operations over the years.*

B: *Oh, yes, what a terrible life – first polio and then that awful accident. It's amazing she produced so many paintings, isn't it?*

A: *Yes, she must have been an incredibly brave woman.*

B: *But the marriage didn't work out too well, did it?*

C: *Well, it had its ups and downs.*

B: *She painted this one with the cropped hair while they were separated, didn't she?*

C: *Yes, that's right.*

B: *She really looks like a man here. In fact, she looks as if she's got a moustache! And why was she dressed in a man's suit?*

A: *I thought it might have had something to do with women's liberation. You know – she cut off her hair to symbolise equality or something.*

C: *Er, no – the reason she cut off her hair and put on a man's suit is because Diego Rivera loved her long hair, and also loved the traditional women's Mexican dresses she used to wear. She did it to hurt him.*

B: *And why did they divorce?*

C: *Er, nobody really knows. Diego may have found out about Frida's affair with Leon Trotsky, or it could have been Frida who was unhappy about Diego's affair with an American film star. What we are sure about is that Frida was very unhappy about the divorce.*

A: *But they were back together by the time she painted 'Roots'.*

C: *Yes, they remarried a year after they separated. She painted this one when her health was beginning to deteriorate. She must have been in a lot of pain.*

B: *I find this one rather depressing. The rocks she's lying on don't look very comfortable – I suppose they represent her pain.*

C: *Probably, but actually, if you look at the expression on her face, she looks quite calm. I think the green leaves suggest hope. In spite of everything, she was a very optimistic person. The last painting she did was called 'Viva la vida' – long live life.*

Collocation (p 91)

1 Students choose the correct words to complete the sentences. Check answers with the class.

a) polio

b) her room

c) seriously

d) underwent

e) surgery

2 Students choose words from the box to replace those in bold.

a) an unknown virus

b) a wheelchair

c) badly

d) survived

e) laser treatment

3 Pairwork. Students talk about other famous people with health problems. They then report back to the class.

Students may know some of the following:

Michael J Fox, star of *Back to the Future* and other movies, suffers from Parkinson's disease and has had to give up acting.

Muhammed Ali, the heavyweight boxer, has also developed Parkinson's disease, probably as a result of being hit on the head during his boxing career.

Rock Hudson, the film star, contracted AIDS and died.

George Best, a former Northern Irish football star, suffers from alcoholism.

The German composer, Beethoven, went deaf in his later years.

The English poet, John Milton, became blind.

Close up (p 92)

Optional activity

Ask your students to look at the pictures. Ask them if they recognise any of them or the styles of painting. Ask them to describe what they can see and to say if they like any of the pictures.

Modals of deduction (p 92)

1 ▭ **48 SB p 154**

Play the recording. Students listen and look at the pictures. Ask them to say which one the people are talking about.

They are talking about picture (c), *Guernica* by Pablo Picasso.

▭ **48**

(A = Alice; B = Bob)

A: *What can you tell me about this picture then?*

B: *Well, I dunno. It looks a bit strange to me. It must be a fairly modern picture. I suppose it might be a Picasso. Wasn't his style something like that? I dunno. To be honest, I don't know a lot about art. Could it be by, oh, wassisname, Salvo Dali, or something?*

A: *All right, what do you think it's about then?*

B: *Who knows! It's a bit hard to make out, isn't it? Is it a man or a woman? OK, say a man. I guess he could be in a prison. Is that a prison bar above his head? I think he may be crying – no, no, hang on, those funny things there must be his nose. Anyway, it's not much good, is it? He can't be much of a painter. Either that, or he must have been in a bit of a hurry. Not my kind of thing, I'm afraid.*

2 Play the recording again. Students complete the phrases.

a) must
b) might
c) could
d) may
e) can't
f) must

3 Whole class. Elicit answers to the questions. If students have problems with modals of deduction, go through the Language reference section on page 93 with them.

a) Sentences *a, e* and *f*.
b) Sentences *b, c* and *d*.
c) Sentence *f*.

4 Pairwork. Students take turns to be A and B, making sentences and guessing which picture the other is talking about.

5 Pairwork. Students turn to page 137 and look at the complete paintings. They discuss which ones they like best.

Optional activity

Before students turn to page 137, ask them to discuss in pairs what they think will be in the rest of the paintings from which these details are taken. They then turn to page 137 and find out how accurate their predictions were.

6 Pairwork. Read the instructions with the whole class before the students work in pairs. You might also like to elicit examples of sentences using *must* and *can't* to express certainty before they begin. Check answers with the class.

a) must
b) can't
c) must
d) can't
e) can't
f) must
g) must

Word linking (p 92)

1 ▭ **49 SB p 92**

Play the recording. Students listen and read the conversation, marking the stresses on the bold sections and completing the last line.

Ann: Well, I <u>must</u> have <u>had</u> them when I came in.
Bob: That's right. So they <u>can't</u> have <u>gone</u> very far.
Ann: Oh, Bob, I <u>can't</u> have <u>lost</u> them, can I?
Bob: No, they <u>must</u> have <u>fallen</u> on the floor where we were sitting.

Ann:	Oh, I can't see them anywhere.
Bob:	Well, someone <u>must</u> have <u>picked</u> them up.
Ann:	They <u>can't</u> have been <u>stolen</u>, can they?
Bob:	No, they <u>must</u> have been <u>handed</u> in at the lost property office.
Ann:	Oh, ... look ... here they are! Under the seat.
Bob:	Huh, you <u>can't</u> have been <u>looking</u> very carefully!
Ann:	Sorry. I can't *see* a thing without my *glasses*!

2 Pairwork. Students practise the conversation, concentrating on linking the words as instructed. It might be a good idea to get several students to demonstrate the linking to the class first.

3 Pairwork. Students make up short conversations speculating about something which has been lost. Encourage a few pairs to perform their conversations for the class.

Eureka (p 93)

Closed books. Ask students if they know what *Eureka* means and who is supposed to have said it? (It means 'I have discovered it' and is supposed to have been said by the Greek scientist Archimedes when he got into his bath, saw the water level rise, and deduced his principle that the volume of water displaced by an object is equal to the volume of the object itself.)

1 Groupwork. Students study the pictures, discuss the order in which the things were invented and try to put a date to each one. They can check their answers on page 139, but encourage them to try to guess all of them before they look at the answers.

f)	The toothbrush (1498)
b)	The toilet (1597)
d)	False teeth (1770)
a)	The contact lens (1887)
e)	The safety razor (1901)
c)	The zip (1913)

2 Still in their groups, students order the inventions according to the criteria given. They then compare their results with other groups.

3 Groups discuss the new inventions and decide which ones would make their lives easier. Students can suggest other imaginative inventions, and the class can vote on the best one.

Listening (p 94)

1   🔲   **50 SB p 155**
Read the information about Trevor Baylis and establish what a clockwork radio is (a radio which doesn't need batteries or electricity; you wind it up like an old-fashioned clock). Then go through the questions with the class.

Play the recording. As they listen, students decide in what order the questions are asked.

Correct order: d, f, b, g, a, e, c

🔲 **50**
Interview with Trevor Baylis
(I = Interviewer; TB = Trevor Baylis)

I: *Trevor, let me, er, start by asking you what gave you the idea for the clockwork radio?*

TB: *Well, I was sitting where I am now looking at that television over there, and I was, um, actually watching a programme about the spread of AIDS in Africa, and they said the only way they could stop this dreadful disease cutting its way through Africa was with the power of information and education. But there was a problem. Most of Africa doesn't have electricity. The only form of electricity available to them was in the form of batteries, which were horrendously expensive. And so I said to myself, hang on, hang on. Now, this is where dreams play an important part in everybody's life. You got to explain what a dream is all about. Um, the beautiful thing about a dream is you can do anything you like in your dreams, right? Now why I am saying this to you is because I could see myself somewhere in the jungle, right? And I can see myself with a pith helmet, a monocle, a gin and tonic in my left hand and one of those fly swatting things, listening to some raunchy number by Dame Nellie Melba on my wind-up gramophone, mmm? And then I am thinking to myself, blimey, if you can get all that noise by dragging a rusty nail around a piece of old bakelite using a spring, surely there's enough power in that spring to drive a small dynamo which in turn will drive my radio, and so I was stirred enough to get off my backside and go to my, my shed, my studio, which sounds so much nicer, my graveyard of a thousand domestic appliances, and actually find enough parts to actually start doing those first primitive experiments ...*

I: *And, um, how long did it take you to design a prototype from the idea ...?*

TB: *Well, from the actual, from the concept to, er, having the first in-a-box model out there it would have taken me two to three months, I guess, so, yes, it took about two or three months.*

I: *So you got, you got the prototype, um, how easy was it from that point on? How easy was it to find a backer and set up production?*

TB: *Well, first things first. I did know that there are these thieves about that will steal your idea. Because I had a whole range of products for the disabled that were stolen from me at an earlier time. So I did know about patents and how important they were. So I found a lady called Jackie Needle, a patent attorney, and I said to her 'Jackie, I want to write up a patent, can you help me?' So we did a search and couldn't find any clockwork radios of the kind that I had done, and she filed for a patent to me, for me, and therefore then I had a starting date, as it were. Now I knew that nobody pays you for a good idea, but they could pay you for that piece of paper, so then I went round every British company I could think of with a confidentiality agreement, and they all talked down to me. 'Oh yes, I think we're, I think that we are working on something like this, aren't we, Johnny?' You know all that old sausage. Um, I mean it was so humiliating ... and in the end, quite frankly after about three or four years of this, I thought, I have had enough of this. Why do I need this? I was fifty-six or something when this happened. So I was given a chance through the BBC World Service to meet up with the guys from the BBC Tomorrow's World programme, and they said, 'Come on, we'll do the story.'*

I: *So the whole thing got off the ground. How long was it then before the production of them started?*

TB: *Well, the important thing was funding. Um, the Tomorrow's World programme was seen by a fellow in South Africa, a chap from a company called Liberty Life. He came to my house here, and we sat out there, and he said 'Look, um, we can help you make this happen, provided we can share in its success.' I said of course, and so we formed a company called Baygen, Baylis Generators, and he wrote a cheque for three-quarters of a million pounds whilst I was in this room.*

I: *And how many radios are produced each month?*

TB: *Well, I'm sure they might tell me differently, but I'm sure they must be doing 200,000 a month.*

I: *And in what ways has the clockwork radio changed your life?*

TB: *Well, not, not significantly. I mean my lifestyle hasn't changed. The house hasn't, has remained more or less the same, but I do get involved with lots more television and radio. I like people, so I'm doing fundamentally what I like doing anyway, communicating.*

I: *And finally what advice would you give to someone who had a good idea?*

TB: *Don't go down the pub and tell everyone about it. That's the first thing, right? Get on to the Patent Office. Get their literature, and read all about it, right? Nobody pays you for a good idea, but they might pay you for a piece of paper which says you own that idea. But remember, somebody might already own that idea, so you must do a search first. There's no excuse afterwards.*

2 Students match Trevor Baylis' responses to the questions in 1.

a) 3   b) 7   c) 1   d) 4   e) 6   f) 2   g) 5

3 Students listen again to the interview and check their answers.

4 Students complete the summary using words from the box. They compare their answers with a partner.

1	spread
2	dream
3	concept
4	prototype
5	filed
6	backer
7	money
8	Baygen
9	lifestyle
10	invention

5 Whole class. Elicit students' opinions of the clockwork radio and find out if they had heard of it before. Then ask for suggestions for the last question. Encourage students who volunteer ideas to say why these products are the most useful.

Word families (p 95)

1 Read the sentence at the top with the class. Ask what part of speech the words in italics are (*inventor* – noun (person); *invention* – noun (thing); *inventive* – adjective).

Students complete the table with the correct words.

1 Noun (study)	2 Noun (person)	3 Adjective +	example collocations
a) science	scientist	scientific	research, advances
b) technology	technologist	technological	advances, research
c) maths	mathematician	mathematical	equations, research

1 Noun (study)	2 Noun (person)	3 Adjective	+ example collocations
d) chemistry	chemist	chemical	reactions, weapons, engineering
e) physics	physicist	physical	health
f) genetics	geneticist	genetic	engineering
g) biology	biologist	biological	weapons
h) economics	economist	economic	growth, research

2 Pairwork. Students underline the stresses. Encourage them to do this by reading the words aloud and deciding what sounds right.

> See underlines in table above.

3 Students use the collocations from 1 to complete the sentences. Check answers with the class.

> 1 mathematical equations
> 2 scientific research
> 3 genetic engineering
> 4 Economic growth
> 5 biological weapons
> 6 Technological advances
> 7 chemical reactions
> 8 physical health

Close up (p 95)

Narrative tense structures

1 Get one of the students to read the sentence aloud. Elicit from the others what the tenses are.

> 1 past continuous
> 2 past simple
> 3 past simple
> 4 past simple
> 5 past perfect

2 Whole class. Discuss the questions. If students have difficulty, go through the Language reference section on page 96 with them.

> a) past simple
> b) past continuous
> c) past perfect

3 Give students time to read and complete the text and to compare answers with a partner.

> 1 In 1977
> 2 Each Sunday
> 3 One Sunday
> 4 a few months previously
> 5 The following day

4 Students choose the correct verb structures.

> 1 was working
> 2 felt
> 3 had been affected
> 4 had heard
> 5 had been installed

5 Students put the words in brackets into the most appropriate form.

> 1 had been demonstrating
> 2 had left
> 3 discovered
> 4 had left
> 5 pulled

Optional activity

Ask students which of the stories about inventions they like most and which was the most surprising.

Trivia pursuit – Genius edition (p 97)

You will need to provide a dice and two counters for each group of players.

Go through the rules with the students and give them time to write their four general knowledge questions. Make sure they understand that they have to be questions to which they know the answers. Go round checking that they are doing this correctly.

Students then play the game.

Test

1 (2 points per correct answer)

1 must be
2 can't be
3 might have gone
4 can't have left
5 must have fallen
6 might be
7 might have got
8 must have left

2
1 look
2 looks/looked like
3 looked as if / as though
4 look
5 looks as if / as though

3
1 was working
2 spotted
3 decided
4 wasn't
5 made
6 had seen
7 had thought
8 began
9 called
10 had changed
11 was employing
12 sold

4
1 technological
2 scientific
3 medical
4 inventive
5 competitive
6 mathematical
7 economic/economical

10 *Genius* Test

Name: Total: _____ /40

---

1 **Modals of deduction** *16 points*

Complete the sentences using *can't, might* or *must* and the correct form of an appropriate verb.

1 I know I put my passport in my bag. It

_____ in here somewhere.

2 At least she passed, so she _____ too disappointed with her exam results.

3 If I hadn't been so tired I _____ to the party.

4 Judy _____ yet. There's her coat.

5 I don't remember the end of that film. I

_____ asleep.

6 James looks very unhappy. Do you think he

_____ homesick?

7 Charlie and Sara are very late. Do you think they

_____ lost?

8 I can't find my umbrella. I think I

_____ it in the taxi.

2 *Look / look like / look as if* *5 points*

Complete the dialogue using the correct form of *look, look like* or *look as if*.

A: Did you see Fiona at the cinema last night? She didn't

(1) _____ very good.

B: I know. She (2) _____ a man in that coat!

A: I didn't mean that. She (3) _____ she'd seen a ghost.

B: Oh, yeah. She did (4) _____ rather pale, didn't she? I suppose she didn't like the film much.

A: It was pretty scary. Do you want to go and see it again tonight?

B: I can't. I'm broke. It (5) _____ I'll have to stay in every night now until pay day!

3 **Narrative tenses** *12 points*

Put the verbs into the past simple, past continuous or past perfect form.

Betty Smith (1) _____ (work) as a

typist when she (2) _____ (spot) a

problem and (3) _____ (decide) to

try to come up with a solution. Unfortunately Betty

(4) _____ (not be) a very good typist

and she (5) _____ (make) a lot of

mistakes. But she (6) _____ (see) the

way house painters covered their mistakes and

(7) _____ (think) of a good idea. In

1951, she (8) _____ (begin) making a

water-based white paint in her garage which she

(9) _____ (call) *Mistake Out*. By 1976

she (10) _____ (change) the name of

the product to *Liquid Paper* and she

(11) _____ (employ) 200 people,

making 25 million bottles per year. Four years later she

(12) _____ (sell) the company to the

Gillette Corporation for $47.5m.

4 **Word families** *7 points*

Form an adjective with each of these nouns.

1 technology _____

2 science _____

3 medicine _____

4 invention _____

5 competition _____

6 mathematics _____

7 economics _____

Photocopiable

11 Sell Overview

The topic of this unit is advertising and the way advertisers manipulate us to make us buy their products. The responsibility of advertisers and the press in general to tell the truth is also examined. The grammar focus is on relative clauses and cleft sentences.

Students begin by identifying and discussing famous brand logos. They then listen to an example of pester power, a child pestering his mother to buy him famous brand trainers. A further listening examines the issues around the exploitation of pester power by advertisers.

The focus then turns to television advertising. Students listen to people describing adverts and match them to pictures. They then talk about adverts that they like. Next, they read a text about a popular television advert for Levis jeans. They match sections of the text to parts of a picture and then discuss how they would make an advert for jeans.

Students then discuss the intrusion of the press into the private lives of celebrities and listen to a radio programme in which a celebrity complains about the lies and inaccuracies printed in the tabloid press about her.

Finally, students look at the hype surrounding the release of the film *The Blair Witch Project* and listen to the views of people who went to see it because of the advance publicity but were disappointed. They then discuss their own experiences of this.

Section	Aims	What the students are doing
Introduction page 98	*Conversation skills*: fluency work	Discussing logos and branded goods.
The playground pound pages 98–99	*Listening skills*: listening for gist and listening for detail	Listening to a child pestering his mother for Nike trainers. Listening to people talking about children and advertising. Matching statements to people and discussing them.
	Lexis: collocations	Completing a text with noun + noun collocations to do with marketing.
Commercials pages 100–102	*Listening skills*: listening for gist	Listening to people talking about TV adverts and identifying the product.
	Conversation skills: fluency work	Discussing commercials.
	Reading skills: reading for detail	Reading a text about a popular TV advert and matching paragraphs to parts of a picture.
	Lexis: words from the reading text	Matching vocabulary items with definitions.
	Speaking skills: discussion	Discussing how to make a TV advert for jeans.
Close up pages 102–103	*Grammar*: relative clauses	Practising the form and use of defining and non-defining relative clauses.
Truth or tabloid? pages 104–105	*Conversation skills*: fluency work	Discussing press intrusion into private lives.
	Listening skills: listening for gist, listening for detail	Listening to a radio programme about truth and accuracy in the tabloid press and explaining the issues discussed.
Close up pages 105–106	*Grammar*: cleft sentences	Changing emphasis by using cleft sentences. Practising stress in cleft sentences.
Hype pages 107–108	*Reading skills*: reading for detail	Reading about the factors which contributed to the success of the film *The Blair Witch Project*.
	Lexis: gradable and absolute adjectives	Using gradable and absolute adjectives correctly to describe degrees of fear.
	Listening skills: listening for gist	Listening to people who have seen the film to determine their general reaction.
	Conversation skills: fluency work	Anecdote: talking about a film which has disappointed you.

11 Sell Teacher's notes

Closed books. At the end of the previous lesson, ask students to bring advertisements from magazines and newspapers to class. Alternatively, bring in a selection of advertisements yourself. In groups students discuss the advertisements and decide who the advertisers are trying to persuade to buy the product (children, adults, women, men, etc.) and how they are doing it (for example, by suggesting that you will be more attractive, socially successful, etc. if you buy it).

Optional activity

Brainstorm some famous brand names and write them on the board. Discuss whether products with famous brand names are better than those which don't have famous brand names.

1 Groupwork. Students look at the six sets of logos, identify them and decide which is the correct one in each case.

> Brands: 1 Head   2 Nike   3 Adidas   4 Speedo
>   5 Slazenger   6 Kappa
> Correct versions: 1 a   2 b   3 a   4 c   5 c   6 b

2 Pairwork. Students discuss the questions. In a feedback session, show the logos that different students have drawn to the class and see if they can identify them or correct them.

The playground pound (p 98)

Closed books. Tell students the title of this section and ask them what they think it means. (In many countries, children have more money than they used to and have become an important target for advertisers. 'The playground pound' refers to this sector of the market: children who have the money to buy products, or who can persuade their parents to buy them.) Ask them if they can guess what the 'grey pound' might be (older people with money).

Listening (p 98)

1 🔲 51 SB p 155

Go through the questions with the class and then play the recording. Elicit answers. You could then ask students whether they think Perry's mother is being unreasonable or not.

> a) About twelve or thirteen.
> b) He wants some new Nike trainers because he wants to look like his cool friends.
> c) He promises not to be rude and to keep his room tidy and not to ask for anything else for Christmas or his birthday.

🔲 **51**

(P = Perry; M = Mum)

P: *Mum, I need a new pair of trainers.*

M: *Okay, I'll give you £20, and you can go and get some.*

P: *£20!!!!! I can't get a pair of trainers for £20!*

M: *Your last pair cost less than that.*

P: *I know, and everybody made fun of me. It's not nice being the odd one out.*

M: *Don't be silly.*

P: *You don't understand. I need Nikes.*

M: *What's so special about Nikes?*

P: *All my friends've got them.*

M: *What, even Jamie?*

P: *Mum, Jamie's pathetic. I mean all my cool friends have got them. And Michael Jordan wears them.*

M: *Who's Michael Jordan?*

P: *Oh honestly, he's only the most famous basketball player ever.*

M: *I am not paying £50 for a pair of trainers.*

P: *£69.99.*

M: *What! I've never spent that much on a pair of shoes.*

P: *Yeah, but you don't care how you look.*

M: *Perry!*

P: *I promise I won't be rude any more, and I'll keep my room tidy, and I won't want anything else for my next birthday or Christmas.*

M: *I'm not spending £70 on a pair of trainers.*

P: *You want me to look stupid, don't you? I hate you.*

2 Pairwork. Students discuss the questions. You may need to explain *pester* (to keep asking someone to buy something for you or do something for you until they finally give in and do it) and *craze* (an enthusiastic but brief interest in something shared by a lot of people).

Optional activity

Ask students how many of the items in the photographs they can identify and find out if they know children who have any of these things. Did these children pester their parents to buy them? Did they want them because their friends had them? Do they still play with them? How long did their interest in them last?

3 Students look at the photographs of the people and read some of the things they say. They then predict which person made each of the statements. Do not check answers at this stage.

4 ▭ **52 SB p 155**

Play the recording for students to listen to and check their answers.

Pairwork. Students discuss the statements in 1 and decide whether they agree or disagree.

a) Sally McIlveen
b) Joe Smedley
c) Sally McIlveen
d) Joe Smedley
e) Joe Smedley
f) Sally McIlveen

▭ **52**

Joe Smedley, marketing executive

Children are much easier to reach with advertising than adults are – they like it and they pick up on it really fast. So, it's the advertiser's job to capitalise on this.

We have a term, 'pester-power', which means the marketing potential of children nagging their parents to spend money. And I'm not just talking about toys here – our aim is getting children to pester parents to buy something for the whole family, like a holiday or car. The trick is to produce adverts that appeal to both children and adults – to split the message in two.

Another key concept for advertisers is 'the playground pound'. Children want what their friends have – playground credibility is very important. In other words, brands give children a sense of identity and help them fit in with a peer group. For instance, if you have the wrong brand of trainers, you're excluded. Brands have the power to show that you're the right sort of kid. If you get it a little bit wrong, it's completely wrong.

So you can see children are a very important market for us, and in return, we like to promote education. In fact we're looking into promoting our products directly in the classroom. This is something that's already happening in America. Companies donate free computers and other school equipment in exchange for advertising their brands on exercise book covers, posters and that sort of thing. I think it's fantastic – the kids benefit, and the companies get brand loyalty from a very early age.

I'd love to be a child today. They really know what they want and they have so many more choices. Advertisers respect children's opinions.

Sally McIlveen, headteacher

Basically, children nowadays are being constantly brainwashed by all the advertising that goes on around them. I tell you what – if the children in my school remembered any of their school work as well as they remember the advertising jingles they hear on television, my job would be a pleasure.

Usually the pupils at our school wear uniforms, but Friday is a non-uniform day, and that's when you really see the power of advertising. The kids are dressed from head to toe in labels, mainly sports stuff like Adidas, Nike, that sort of thing. And they all look the same!

There's a great deal of pressure on parents to buy children all these labels and gadgets. They call it 'pester power' – children nag their parents until they give in. I feel sorry for the families who don't have much money, because the pressure is just the same.

I really believe it's time the government put a stop to all this aggressive television advertising.

Mind you, it's worse in America apparently. Schools are actually being subsidised by companies like McDonalds and Pepsi. Okay, the school gets free equipment from these big companies, but then the children have to add up burgers or multiply cans of Pepsi in their maths lessons. I think it's terrible to think that the schools end up promoting a product that's not even good for the children. I mean, where will it end? Will we see the day when kids are required to wear Nikes before they're allowed to go to school?

Companies like to say they're promoting education and school-business partnerships, but what they're really doing is going after the kids' market wherever they can.

I think it's really sad that children are being forced to be consumers from such an early age. I don't think all this choice is liberating for children – it just means that they're getting older younger, and that's a shame.

Lexis (p 99)

1 Read the introduction with the whole class, then ask students to work individually to make fifteen noun + noun collocations. Check answers with the class.

a) sales
b) brand
c) market
d) consumer
e) advertising

2 Pairwork. Students match the collocations they have made with the dictionary definitions. Check answers with the class.

a) market research

b) brand name

c) sales pitch

d) consumer goods

e) sales force

f) market forces

3 Students can write their sentences alone and then compare them with a partner.

Commercials (p 100)

Listening

1 53 SB p 156

Students look at the pictures and identify the products being advertised. Make sure they understand that the speakers on the recording will talk about television advertisements for only four of the products illustrated.

Play the recording. Students listen and match the advertisements being described with four of the pictures.

Alison: f   Ben: e   Celia: a   Dan: c

53

Alison

My favourite one is the one where this guy invites his girlfriend back to his flat for a drink. He's a typical lazy slob, and the flat is a right mess as they walk in, and he tries to tidy up a few things. Erm, then, he goes into the kitchen but he finds he's run out, except for a jar of instant. So he starts making funny noises, like, er, ssh, sshh, brrr, sshh. He opens up cupboards and closes them, pretending he's really busy. After a few minutes he comes out, and she believes it's the real thing. Mind you, if she's stupid enough to be going out with a guy like that, she'd probably believe anything.

Ben

I saw one the other day that I really liked. It was a sunny day in a park, and there's this kind of angel character flying around all over the place. You know, a sort of Cupid with a bow and arrow. He keeps firing arrows at people but he keeps missing, or he shoots a dog which falls in love with an old lady or something. And he's getting really dejected 'cos he's getting it all wrong, when this other Cupid turns up, but instead of shooting love arrows, he fires these vanilla cones at people. So, there's a couple on the bench having an argument, when all of a sudden, they're both holding cones and all in love with each other. I scream when I see that one ... Get it? I scream ... Oh, never mind.

Celia

There was another one years ago that was really good. It was always the same bloke, and, erm, terrible things kept happening to him. Like, em, he'd be in a sinking ship and the water would be coming up to his knees, or he was painting a room and he finds he's painted himself into a corner and he can't move. Oh, I don't know, there were loads of different situations, and each time it was really terrible. But instead of getting depressed, he'd take one look at the situation and he'd put his hand in his pocket, take one out and light up. Then he would blow out the smoke and smile, looking really relaxed.

Dan

Do you remember that one with a sort of James Bond kind of character who parachutes onto the roof of a skyscraper? He's got a coil of rope over one shoulder and a package strapped to his back. Then he jumps over the edge of the roof and abseils down the building. Then, when he's gone down ten floors or so he smashes through the window with his feet. Then what? Oh, yeah, there's this beautiful woman in the room, who looks up at him, but without being too surprised. He takes the package off his back and he gets down on his knees. He opens it up and hands it over to the gorgeous woman. Er, that's it, I think. Do you remember that one?

2 Pairwork. Students take turns to describe advertisements without saying the name of the product. The listening student each time has to guess what was being advertised. They should ask questions to get more information if necessary.

3 Pair or groupwork. Students discuss their favourite and least favourite advertisements. They decide which advertisements are most effective and report back to the class on their discussions.

Reading (p 100)

1 Pairwork. Students look at the picture on page 101 and discuss their answers to the questions. Do not check answers at this stage.

2 Students read the first paragraph of the text and check their answers. Check with the class.

a) Jeans.

b) America; 1950s.

3 Students read the rest of the text and match the paragraphs with the numbered parts of the picture. Allow them to compare answers in pairs before checking with the class.

A 1   B 4   C 5   D 2   E 3

4 Students work individually to answer the questions. Allow them to compare notes in pairs or small groups before checking with the class.

> a) It was a massive success.
> b) It was made by a British creative director for a British advertising agency with British actors.
> c) Young, sexy, cool people.
> d) Because of his 1950s heart-throb looks.
> e) A man (rather than a woman) was the object of sexual desire.
> f) Elvis used to wear them. Marvin Gaye's song, *I Heard It Through The Grapevine*, was the sound track to the ad.

Lexis (p 102)

1 Students can work individually or in pairs to find the expressions in the text and match them with the correct definitions. Check answers with the class.

> a) is a typical example of
> b) creates a picture of
> c) very concerned about details
> d) a very attractive man
> e) is not at all interested in

2 Make sure students understand they may have to make some changes to fit the expressions into the sentences. Check answers with the class.

> a) conjure up
> b) heart-throb
> c) couldn't care less about
> d) epitomises
> e) fussy

3 Pairwork. Students take turns to ask and answer the questions in 2.

Discussion (p 102)

1 Groupwork. Students discuss the questions. Give them plenty of time to do this.

2 Groupwork. Groups compare their ideas.

Optional activity

If you have the facilities, you could ask students to produce videos of their jeans advertisements.

Close up (p 102)

Relative clauses

1 Elicit a few examples of relative clauses from the class to check that they remember what they are. If they are unsure, go through the Language reference section on page 103 with them. Students then underline the relative clauses in the extracts.

> a) which was perfect for Levis' intended positioning of their brand in the market
> b) who was creative director of the London-based agency, Bartle Bogle Hegarty
> c) that are hanging out of the machine

2 Ask students to tell you which description fits each of the relative clauses in 1.

> a 3   b 1   c 2

3 Check that students understand the difference between defining and non-defining relative clauses (this is explained in the Language reference on page 103). They then look again at the extracts in 1 and answer the question.

> Commas.

4 Pairwork. Students decide which follow-up sentence goes with each main sentence. Check answers with the class.

> a 1   b 2   c 2   d 1   e 2   f 1   g 1   h 2

5 Whole class. Read out each main sentence in 4 and elicit answers to the questions.

> a)   a: Type 2 (defining)
>   b: Type 3 (non-defining)
>   c: Type 1 (non-defining)
>   d: Type 3 (non-defining)
>   e: Type 2: (defining)
>   f: Type 3 (non-defining)
>   g: Type 2 (defining)
>   h: Type 1 (non-defining)
> b)   that

6 Go through the instructions with the class. Make sure they understand that they are to form defining relative clauses and that there is one extra word in each. Students work individually to make the clauses and identify the extra word. You may like to point out that in formal English, it would be more correct in c) and h) to say *a boss with whom you get on* and *a partner with whom you are in love*.

> a) a job that you are interested in ~~it~~
> b) a bank account that ~~it~~ never runs out
> c) a boss who you get on with ~~him/her~~

d) a car that ~~it~~ never breaks down

e) a government that you voted for ~~them~~

f) a friend who ~~he/she~~ never lets you down

g) a home that you are happy in ~~there~~

h) a partner who you are in love with ~~him/her~~ .

7 Elicit answers to the questions from the class.

> You can't omit *that* when it's the subject of the relative clause. You can only omit it when it's the object.
>
> You can omit the relative pronoun in a, c, e, g, h.

8 Pairwork. Students decide on their order of importance. Allow them to compare their results with other pairs.

Truth or tabloid? (p 104)

Closed books. Ask students if they believe everything they read in the newspapers. If they say that they don't, ask them for examples of things they have read in a paper which they either didn't believe or which subsequently turned out to be untrue. If they say they do believe everything they read in the press, ask them if all newspapers are equally reliable.

1 Pairwork. Students discuss the questions and report back to the class.

2 Students read the article. Ask them if they feel sorry for Phil Bronstein and for Sharon Stone.

3 Ask students to say which untrue story they would find most upsetting.

Listening (p 105)

1 📼 **54 SB p 156**

Pairwork. Go through the instructions with the class and play the recording. Students then work in pairs to explain why the actress is unhappy with the editor.

Bring the class back together to talk about who they sympathise with most. Encourage students who give their opinions to explain why they sympathise with a particular person. Have a class vote to find out who students sympathise with most.

> The tabloid editor's newspaper said that Shelley and her co-star had taken a bath together in her hotel room. The co-star is married to a good friend of Shelley's. The newspaper said the bath was filled with $5,000 worth of champagne. Shelley's co-star's wife is filing for a divorce.

📼 **54**

(P = Presenter; S = Shelley Russell; J = Jim Falmer)

P: *Good evening and welcome to Talkback. Recently, the tabloid press have been under fire yet again, this time for their apparent disregard for truth and accuracy.*

In the studio tonight we would like to welcome Shelley Russell, Oscar-winning actress, and Jim Falmer, editor of The Daily Post. Shelley Russell, let's start with you. Do you think there should be greater restrictions placed on the press and the stories they print?

S: *Yes, absolutely. I can't open a newspaper or magazine without reading stories full of false information about myself or people I know. It's getting ...*

J: *Sorry, but I can't believe that you're actually complaining about free publicity. I mean, I remember, Shelley, before you were famous, you were begging us to write features about you ... anything ...*

S: *If you would just let me finish – of course the press have been important. I'm an actress and I understand the power of the press. But the thing is, I rarely seem to read anything true about myself these days. Take last week – your paper wrote this story about me and my co-star, who incidentally happens to be married to a very good friend of mine – taking a bath together in my hotel room.*

J: *Oh that. That was ...*

S: *Hang on, I haven't finished. You went on to say that the bath was filled with $5,000 worth of champagne. Now, ...*

J: *Well, that was just a bit of fun. I don't think you should take that too seriously.*

S: *Oh really! You don't think that it's at all serious that my co-star's children woke up to the headline: SHELLEY GETS BUBBLY WITH SHAUN IN CHAMPAGNE BATH, or that his wife is now filing for a divorce ...*

J: *Look, I don't know whether ...*

S: *Anyway, to get back to what I was saying ... The point I'm trying to make here is that famous people have families with feelings. I am sick of the gutter-press making up stories just so that they can splash sensational headlines across the front page and sell more newspapers – it's irresponsible and it messes up people's lives.*

J: *Look love, you're just angry about that particular article because the photos we printed of you weren't very flattering. Anyway, we made a public apology and said that there'd been some inaccuracies in the article.*

S: *Yes, but what you didn't do was say what the inaccuracies were, so ...*

P: *If I could just come in here. I think we need to address the root of the problem. Jim Falmer, why do certain newspapers continue to print these stories when it's obvious that they're not true?*

S: To increase circulation and make more money.

J: If you would let me answer the question – I think we have to look at the relationship between fame, the public and the press. The public are fascinated by fame and scandal, and they love to read about their favourite stars. The problem is, it's not always clear what's true and what isn't. I mean, if a newspaper prints something scandalous or embarrassing about a famous person, they're bound to deny it, but that doesn't mean it's not true.

S: Are you trying to say ...

J: No smoke without fire, if you ask me.

P: Well, I'm sorry to interrupt you, but we'll carry on after this short break for some travel news ...

2 Students complete the phrases with the words in the box. If you like, you could play the recording again to help them. Check answers with the class.

a) but
b) finish
c) is
d) on
e) saying
f) is
g) was
h) here
i) question
j) is
k) but

3 Write the headings on the board and ask students to say which column to write the phrases in. Do not clean the board before the next exercise.

Interrupting	Returning to the topic	Introducing a new point
Sorry, but ...	If you would just let me finish ...	But the thing is ...
Hang on, ...	Anyway, to get back to what I was saying ...	The point I'm trying to make here is ...
If I could just come in here ...	If you would let me answer the question ...	What you didn't do was ...
I'm sorry to interrupt you, but ...		The problem is ...

4 Groupwork. Students discuss the statements. Encourage them to look at the board and use the phrases in their discussions.

Close up (p 105)

Emphasis (cleft sentences)

1 Ask two students to read the first two sentences aloud. Then get another pair to read the second two sentences. Ask students if they contain the same information and to say what the difference between them is. Then go through the Language reference section on page 106 with the class.

> The second two sentences have the structure *What ... is* which gives much greater emphasis to one part of the sentence.

2 Students work individually to change the emphasis in the sentences. Check answers with the class.

> a) What I don't understand is why I never have any money.
>
> b) The thing I like about weekends is I can stay in bed late in the morning.
>
> c) What really annoys me is people who finish my sentences for me.
>
> d) What I feel like doing tonight is going to the cinema.
>
> e) The thing I hate about winter is it gets dark so early.
>
> f) What I'd really like to do is live abroad in the future.

3 Pairwork. Students decide which statements in 2 are true for them and discuss with a partner.

4 Allow students to discuss the statements in pairs or groups and decide which one is true.

> Statement c is true.

5 Pairwork. Students correct the false statements in 4. Go round making sure they are using the expressions *It was ...* or *It wasn't ...* correctly.

> a) It wasn't Anna Kournikova who was attacked by a mad fan during a match. It was Monica Seles.
>
> b) It wasn't Tom Cruise who Julia Roberts starred with in *Notting Hill*. It was Hugh Grant.
>
> d) It wasn't Ricky Martin who had a big hit with a song called 'Angels'. It was Robbie Williams.
>
> e) It wasn't Gwyneth Paltrow who got married to Brad Pitt in 2000. It was Jennifer Aniston.
>
> f) It wasn't Leonardo DiCaprio who was Obi-Wan Kenobi in *Star Wars Episode 1: The Phantom Menace*. It was Ewan McGregor.

6 Students can work in pairs to write their sentences. Explain that they shouldn't just write lies about celebrities, but statements similar to those in 4 where the wrong name has been used to describe an event that actually happened. They then pass them to other students who have to discuss what is wrong with them and, if possible, correct them.

Stress in cleft sentences (p 106)

1 🔲 **55 SB p 106**

Read the instructions with the class. Students decide which are the important words in the sentences. Then play the recording so they can hear if those words are stressed or not. They should also mark the pauses.

> a) <u>What</u> I <u>love</u> about <u>Peter</u> … is his <u>wicked sense</u> of <u>humour</u>.
>
> b) The <u>thing</u> I <u>can't stand</u> about <u>this country</u> … is the <u>weather</u>.
>
> c) <u>What</u> I <u>really hate</u> about my <u>job</u> … is <u>having</u> to <u>work</u> at <u>weekends</u>.
>
> d) The <u>person</u> I <u>really like</u> in <u>this class</u> … is <u>Maria</u>.
>
> e) <u>What</u> I find <u>annoying</u> about <u>politicians</u> … is that they <u>never give</u> a <u>straight answer</u>.
>
> f) The <u>thing</u> I find <u>difficult</u> about <u>English</u> … is the <u>spelling</u>.
>
> g) <u>What</u> I would <u>really like</u> to <u>do</u> … is to <u>take</u> a <u>year off</u>.
>
> h) The <u>thing</u> that I <u>respect most</u> about my <u>boss</u> … is her <u>generosity</u>.

2 Pairwork. Students take turns to finish the sentences and give their opinions.

Hype (p 107)

Books closed. Ask students if they have ever bought something or gone to see something at the cinema because they read or heard lots of reports about how good it was? Ask them how they felt about it afterwards. Were they pleased or disappointed?

1 Read the explanation of *hype* with the students. Ask them for examples of things that have been hyped in their country.

Pairwork. Students discuss the questions.

2 Pairwork. Students think about how to make a film hugely successful and add other factors to the list.

> *Possible answers*
> a good director, clever marketing/publicity, a tie-in with a popular book, a sequel to a successful first film, enthusiastic reviews

3 Find out if anyone has seen *The Blair Witch Project*. If they have, ask them why they decided to go and see it and encourage them to tell the others about it. Find out if it was hyped in their country and whether it lived up to their expectations or not.

Students read the article and see if any of the points they listed in 2 are mentioned.

4 Whole class. Ask students to list the factors mentioned in the article which were responsible for the film's success.

> The actors are believable because there wasn't a script and they weren't known.
>
> The website support and the marketing built up anticipation.
>
> The documentary called *The Curse of the Blair Witch* was shown on American TV, producing ambiguity as to whether the story was real or not.
>
> The film opened in only a few cinemas, which created extra media and audience interest and tension.

5 Pairwork. Students discuss the questions and report back to the class.

Lexis (p 108)

1 🔲 **56 SB p 157**

Play the recording. Students listen and choose the correct options.

> a) a bit nervous
> b) a little uneasy
> c) frightened to death
> d) scared stiff
> e) quite apprehensive
> f) absolutely terrified

🔲 **56**
(I = Interviewer; W = Woman; M = Man)

a)

I: *Excuse me. Do you mind if I ask you how you feel about seeing this movie?*

W1: *Um, a bit nervous, actually. I don't know quite what to expect, but I think I'm going to be scared.*

b)

I: *Excuse me – are you feeling nervous about seeing 'The Blair Witch Project'?*

M1: *Yeah, a little uneasy, I must admit … but I've brought my girlfriend, so I can hold her hand if I get scared.*

c)

I: *How do you feel about seeing this movie?*

M2: *I'm looking forward to being frightened to death.*

d)

I: *What are you expecting from this film?*

W2: *To be scared stiff – hopefully.*

e)

I: *Do you think you're going to enjoy 'The Blair Witch Project'?*

W3: *Er, no – I don't think 'enjoy' is the right word. But I've heard so much about it that I can't wait to find out what it's all about. In fact, I feel quite apprehensive, but I love horror films, and this one sounds as if it's going to be really scary.*

f)

I: *Any expectations?*

M3: *Well, I've been visiting the website for a while now and I'm really looking forward to finding out what happens. I expect to be absolutely terrified!*

2 Look at the example with the class. Make sure students understand that for each item in 1, one of the remaining choices forms a collocation with the final word and one of them does not. They must cross out the words that does not collocate. They then write example sentences with the other words.

> a) ~~totally~~ / extremely nervous
> b) distinctly / ~~utterly~~ uneasy
> c) scared / ~~nervous~~ to death
> d) ~~afraid~~ / bored stiff
> e) ~~completely~~ / terribly apprehensive
> f) quite / ~~very~~ terrified

3 Whole class. Establish that gradable adjectives are those which describe something which can vary in intensity (for example *big, funny*). Absolute adjectives describe something unchanging (for example *enormous, hilarious*).

Pairwork. Students look at the sentence frames and decide which adjectives go with which and how the meaning of *quite* changes.

> a) Sentence frame A: interesting, boring, disappointing, entertaining, funny, good,
>
> Sentence frame B: amazing, brilliant, dreadful, extraordinary, spectacular, ridiculous
>
> b) In A, *quite* means *fairly* or *rather*.
>
> In B, *quite* means *completely* or *absolutely*.

4 Students use adverb and adjective expressions from 3 to tell each other about things they have seen recently.

5 🔲 **57 SB p 157**

Play the recording. Students listen and say what the general reaction to the film was.

> They were disappointed.

🔲 **57**

(I = Interviewer; W = Woman; M = Man)

I: *So, how was it for you?*

W1: *Extremely disappointing. I wasn't the least bit scared, and, and you know from the start that everybody dies, so there's no suspense. Anyway, the characters are so annoying that I felt like killing them myself. It does not live up to the hype.*

I: *What did you think of it then?*

M1: *Absolute rubbish. My girlfriend fell asleep, and I spent the last half of the movie with my eyes shut – not because it was scary – but because the camera angles made me feel sick. Don't see it if you suffer from motion sickness. In fact, just don't see it.*

I: *So were you frightened to death?*

M2: *No way. After all the hype, it was a massive letdown.*

I: *What did you think?*

W2: *Over-hyped nonsense. I spent most of the time waiting for something to happen. I feel completely disillusioned.*

I: *Did the film live up to your expectations?*

W3: *No, it didn't. I don't think I've ever been so bored in my entire life, and I still haven't got a clue what it's about. In fact, there's no story to speak of. This film is a perfect example of hype over substance.*

I: *Your verdict?*

M3: *A total waste of time. I was bored out of my mind. The website was much more entertaining than the film.*

6 Students try to remember the speakers' exact words. Allow them to discuss this in pairs or groups and when they have had enough time to make their decisions, play the recording again for them to check their answers.

> a) (1) Extremely (2) the hype
> b) (3) Absolute
> c) (4) massive
> d) (5) completely
> e) (6) entire
> f) (7) total

Anecdote (p 108)

(See the Introduction on page 4 for more ideas on how to set up, monitor and repeat 'anecdotes'.)

Pairwork. Give students time to decide what they are going to talk about and to read through the questions. They then take turns to tell each other about disappointing films. Encourage them to report back to the class on anything interesting that they heard.

Test

Scoring: one point per correct answer unless otherwise indicated.

1
1 which
2 who
3 whose
4 which
5 who
6 whose
7 which
8 which

2 (2 points per correct answer)
1 Jacky is a friend *who* never lets me down.
2 That's Sandra, *whose* mother works in the library.
3 She's got a friend *who* she's known for ages.
4 It's a book *which* I've always wanted to read.
5 I've just seen the boy *whom* I met at the party.
6 Josy's mum, *who* lives next door, sometimes gives us a lift to school.

3 (2 points per correct answer)
1 What
2 that
3 is
4 It
5 what
6 how

4
1 research
2 campaign
3 pitch
4 loyalty

5
1 effects
2 entertaining
3 ridiculous
4 hype

11 *Sell* Test

1   Relative pronouns *8 points*
Complete the sentences with *who, which* or *whose*.

1   There's the car _____ I was telling you about.

2   I'm trying to find somebody _____ will look after the dog while we're on holiday.

3   Jane's the one _____ friend used to go out with a famous singer.

4   Des told me something _____ I'll never forget.

5   I've been talking to Jo, _____ works with Pat.

6   My friend, _____ mother works at the cinema, got us free tickets.

7   She always arrives half an hour late, _____ makes me mad.

8   We bought a house _____ overlooks the sea.

2   Relative clauses *12 points*
Correct the mistakes.

1   Jacky is a friend which never lets me down.

2   That's Sandra, who's mother works in the library.

3   She's got a friend which she's known for ages.

4   It's a book who I've always wanted to read.

5   I've just seen the boy which I met at the party.

6   Josy's mum, that lives next door, sometimes gives us a lift to work.

3   Cleft sentences *12 points*
Complete the dialogue with appropriate words.

A: (1) _____ I love about this place is that you can buy anything you could possibly think of.

B: I know. It's the selection of food from all over the world (2) _____ I really like.

A: Yeah, that's great, but what I really like

(3) _____ the toy department. All those brilliant new electronic games from America.

B: I know. (4) _____ wasn't until recently that you could get any of that stuff over here.

A: Mm, (5) _____ I don't understand is

(6) _____ they manage to stock so many different products in one shop.

4   Vocabulary – collocations *4 points*
Complete the sentences with an appropriate word.

1   Many companies do market r_____ to find out what consumers want.

2   The advertising c_____ featured several big film stars.

3   He's got such a persuasive sales p_____ he could sell anything to anybody.

4   Brand l_____ is when you buy the same make of a product again and again.

5   Vocabulary – films and adjectives *4 points*
Complete the sentences with an appropriate word.

1   The special e_____ in the film were so realisti< that people thought the dinosaurs were real.

2   The film was so e_____ that we decided to se< it again last night.

3   It was a completely r_____ story. Life just isn' like that.

4   There were so much h_____ before the film came out, I got sick of hearing about it.

12 *Student* Overview

The topics of this unit are various aspects of students' lives. The grammar focus is on future forms.

The unit begins with school and an examination of pop star Robbie Williams' memories of school. Students listen to two people talking about particular teachers they remember and then talk about their own favourite teachers. They read stories of people who proved their teachers' predictions wrong.

Students listen to two parents discussing their daughter's plans and then read her point of view. They discuss who they agree with.

Students then read some travellers' tales from a student who has gone backpacking. They see how exaggerated language can make stories more exciting.

Students then look at some tips for writing a CV and find and correct the faults in a badly-written one. They compare a written character reference and a conversation in which two people discuss the person's character.

Finally, they complete the lyrics of the song *Angels* by Robbie Williams and discuss how he felt when he wrote it and what effect it has on them.

Section	Aims	What the students are doing
Introduction page 109	*Conversation skills*: fluency work	Working in pairs to decide on lists of qualities that make good teachers and students.
Could do better pages 109–110	*Reading skills*: reading for detail; reading for gist	Reading a text about pop star Robbie Williams' school life.
	Listening skills: listening for gist and listening for detail	Listening to two people talking about teachers they remember from their schooldays.
	Conversation skills: fluency work	Anecdote: talking about a favourite teacher.
Teachers and parents know best pages 111–112	*Lexis*: collocations	Practising using collocations about school life.
	Reading skills: reading for gist	Reading more stories of people who proved their teachers wrong.
	Listening skills: listening for gist	Listening to Mr and Mrs Barrington discussing their daughter Saffron's future plans.
Close up pages 113–114	*Grammar*: future forms	Using an interview with Saffron to choose appropriate future forms.
		Completing a table of future forms.
Backpacking pages 115–116	*Reading skills*: reading for detail	Reading different versions of stories to see how dramatic language can make them more exciting.
	Lexis: exaggerated language	Practising making texts more exciting by using exaggerated language.
Job hunting pages 117–118	*Writing skills*: CVs	Identifying the mistakes in a CV and rewriting it correctly.
	Listening skills: listening for detail	Listening to a discussion of someone's character and comparing it to a written character reference.
Angels page 119	Song	Completing the lyrics of a Robbie Williams song and discussing the frame of mind in which it was written and the effect it has on the listener.

12 *Student* Teacher's notes

Closed books. Ask students to write down five subjects and five sports they did at school. Students should number each subject and each sport 1–5 according to how good/bad they were at the subject/sport (1 = very bad; 5 = very good). Students work in pairs and tell each other about their performance in the subjects and sports.

For example: *I was really good at maths but I was useless at English.*

Students review the dependent preposition *at* following adjectives describing ability.

Could do better (p 109)

Closed books. Ask students whether their school sends/sent reports to their parents with comments from each teacher saying how they were doing. If so, ask them what kind of comments the teachers make/made. Explain that *Could do better*, the heading of this section, is a common comment made by teachers on British school reports if the student is not terrible but is not working very hard.

Reading (p 109)

1 Ask students what they know about Robbie Williams and go through the information in the margin with them. Ask them what kind of student they think he was. Students then read the text to see if they were right.

2 Students choose the correct alternatives. Check answers with the class.

> 1 a 2 b 3 b 4 a 5 a 6 c

Listening (p 110)

1 📼 58 SB p 157

Students look at the illustrations and discuss in pairs or groups what kind of people they show.

Play the recording. Students listen and match the descriptions to the pictures. Allow them to compare answers in pairs before checking with the class.

> John: c
> Clare: a

📼 58

John

Ah, Madame Lorenzo! How could I ever forget? It was my last year at school, and she took us for French, which I was hopeless at. I remember the

first time she walked into the room. She stood at the front, put her bag down on the teacher's desk and looked around the room. Then she pointed at me and said 'You, boy, take that imbécilic grin off your face. The only thing that's funny is your score in the French exam last year.' Then she started looking around in her big bag and eventually produced a little compact mirror and a lipstick. She held up the mirror, and we could see her long, long fingernails which were the same blood red as the lipstick she started to put on. She must have been near to retirement, but she was incredibly elegant. She was slim and petite with blond hair tied in a tight bun – all the guys in the class were completely fascinated by her. But she was vicious. She had this way of criticising you that made everyone else in the class laugh at you. I can't remember the number of times she reduced me to tears. Every time I hear the word 'imbecile' I still think of her. It was her catchphrase. 'You are an im-bé-cile, boy. I 'ave more brains in my little finger than you have in your 'ole 'ead. You are like my Marcel. You will never amount to much. You are an imbécile.' We all knew that Marcel was her husband, and everyone giggled. I was terrified of going to her classes, but in a funny sort of way I really loved being there.*

Clare

Mr Tucker is the one I remember best. The sergeant, we called him, because he used to wear his military medals to school every day. In fact he always wore the same jacket – in two years I never saw him wear anything else. He had a big moustache and a nervous tic with his eye which twitched really fast when he got angry. He was always shouting as if we were deaf or something. 'You'll learn,' he used to shout. 'You'll learn when you've settled down and started a family. It's not all rubbish that we teach you here, you know.' Another one of his sayings was 'In my day …' 'In my day, young people had to join the army. That used to knock some sense into them. My generation never had the chance to go to university like you lot.' I reckon he was probably too stupid to get into university anyway. A bit sad really. I wonder what he's doing now?

2 Allow students to read through the sentences and discuss who they think each refers to before you play the recording.

Then play the recording for students to mark the sentences. Check answers with the class.

a) ML
b) MT
c) ML
d) ML
e) MT
f) MT
g) ML
h) ML

3 Students complete the sentences with the expressions from the box. Allow them to compare answers in pairs before checking with the class.

a) reduce (their students) to tears
b) amount to much
c) settle down
d) join the army
e) have the chance

Anecdote (p 110)

(See the Introduction on page 4 for more ideas on how to set up, monitor and repeat 'anecdotes'.)

Pairwork. You could start this off by telling the students about your favourite teacher at school. Give them time to go through the questions and think about what they are going to say. They then take turns to describe their teachers.

Teachers and parents know best
(p 111)

Closed books. Ask students if they think that teachers and parents know best. Find out if their parents or teachers have ever given them advice that they rejected at the time but later found out was good advice.

Lexis (p 111)

1 Students work individually to form questions. Check answers.

a 2 b 5 c 8 d 1 e 4 f 6 g 3 h 7

2 Pairwork. Students ask each other the questions in 1. Encourage them to report back any interesting information to the class.

3 Go through the questions with the class before they read the text. Then ask for the answers.

a) Ann Waterman.
b) Henry Woods.
c) Romy Adams.

4 Direct students attention to the expressions in bold in 1.

Ask them to read the texts again and find which two are not used.

get a grant for further education
apply for a place at university

5 Students scan the texts to find matching expressions.

Text 1: *She is bound to* fail the exam.
Text 2: *She is unlikely to* go on to further education..
Text 3: *Henry is not expected to* pass his exams with sufficiently high grades.

6 Go through the predictions one by one with the class asking students to complete them and then discuss whether they will happen in their country and, if so, when.

a) are expected to
b) is highly unlikely
c) are likely to
d) are bound to

7 Pairwork. Students write three more predictions about education in their country. They then exchange them with other pairs and find out if they agree. Students from different nationalities can say whether or not such a thing has already happened in their country or whether they think it is likely to happen.

Listening (p 112)

1 Groupwork. Students discuss the questions. See if there is agreement across the class about the ages in (a).

2 **59 SB p 157**

Before students listen to the recording, you might like to explain something about the education system in Britain.

The school leaving age in Britain is 16. At this age students can leave to get a job. Most take exams called GCSEs first. However, many students stay on after their GCSEs, either at school or at a sixth form college, for a further two years and specialise in three, or sometimes four, subjects. At the end of the two years they take A-level (Advanced level) exams. If they get good enough grades in their A-levels, they can go on to university.

Read the summary sentences with the class before you play the recording. Then ask them which one best summarises Mr and Mrs Barrington's feelings.

Sentence b is the best summary.

59
(I = Interviewer; Mrs B = Mrs Barrington;
Mr B = Mr Barrington)

I: *What's Saffron going to do when she leaves school?*

Mrs B:	*Until a few months ago, she was going to go to university, but she's changed her mind. Now she reckons she's going to make it in the pop world.*
I:	*And how do you feel about that?*
Mr B:	*We think she's making an enormous mistake.*
I:	*But surely she can go back to her studies if her music career fails?*
Mr B:	*That's true, but once she gets a taste of freedom, she'll find it more difficult to go back to college. I just think it's such a waste – in three years' time, she'll have got her degree and she'll still be young enough to try out the music business. At least if it doesn't work out she'll have a qualification behind her.*
I:	*Have you discussed this with her?*
Mrs B:	*Of course, but she's made up her mind. We're just hoping that she'll get it out of her system and then come to her senses and go back to her studies. When I left school I didn't go on to university, and I've regretted it ever since. I just don't want her to make the same mistake as I did.*
I:	*Will you support her while she's trying to be a pop singer?*
Mr B:	*You mean financially? No. She won't be living at home, and we can't afford to pay for her to live in London, so it's up to her to make it work.*

3 Read the expressions in the box with the class. Then play the recording again. Students put the correct phrases in the sentences.

a)	make it
b)	taste of freedom
c)	behind her
d)	out of her system
e)	up to her

4 Pairwork. Students discuss the statements and say what they think their parents' opinions would be.

Close up (p 113)

Future forms

1 Students read the interview with Saffron and choose the appropriate future forms. Allow students to compare with a partner but don't check answers at this stage.

2 ▭ **60 SB p 158**
Play the recording for students to listen to and check their answers. They then discuss whether they agree with Saffron or her parents. Ensure they give reasons for their opinions.

1	my A-levels start
2	I'm going to concentrate
3	I'm going to be
4	I'm going to find
5	I'm moving
6	you'll be able
7	we might have to
8	it's going to be
9	we'll have had
10	I'll be staying
11	I'll give
12	it'll be

▭ **60**
(I = Interviewer; S = Saffron)

I:	*You're leaving school soon, aren't you?*
S:	*Yes, my A-levels start next week, but I'm not too bothered about the results, because when I leave school I'm going to concentrate on my music career. I'm lead singer in a band and I don't need any qualifications to be a pop star. I see my future very clearly – I'm going to be incredibly famous and fabulously rich.*
I:	*So you've already got a contract then?*
S:	*Er, no, not as such. Actually, we haven't got a manager yet, but the minute I've taken my last exam, I'm going to find a really good one.*
I:	*So, do you intend to continue living at home?*
S:	*No way. I'm moving to London just as soon as I've left school. London's where it all happens in the music industry.*
I:	*Do you think you'll be able to live off your music right from the start?*
S:	*Well, if we don't make it straight away we might have to get part-time jobs for a few months or something. I know it's going to be hard at first, but I bet you, by this time next year, we'll have had a record in the charts.*
I:	*And where do you see yourself in five years from now?*
S:	*In five years' time I'll be staying in posh hotels and won't be able to walk down the street without being recognised. In fact, I'll give you my autograph now if you like – it'll be worth a fortune in a few years' time!*

3 Pairwork. Students copy the table and complete it with the names of future forms and examples from the interview. If they have difficulty with this, go through the Language reference section on page 114 with the class. Otherwise encourage them to use it to check their answers.

a) ... it'll be worth a fortune in a few years' time!

b) We might have to get part-time jobs for a few months or something.

c) (be) going to; I'm going to concentrate on my music career.

d) I'm moving to London just as soon as I've left school.

e) Present simple

f) I'll be staying in posh hotels.

g) Future perfect

4 Pairwork. Before students mark the main and subordinate clauses and the conjunctions, go through the example with the class to ensure they understand what each item is. When they have finished this, they discuss the three questions. Check answers with the class.

a) (...(the minute) I've taken my last exam,) I'm going to find a really good one.

b) ... I'm moving to London ((just as soon as) I've left school).

c) ... ((if) we don't make it straight away) we might have to get part-time jobs ...

1 The main clause.

2 No.

3 The subordinate clause.

5 Whole class. Ask individual students to complete the sentences and get the rest of the class to say whether they are right or wrong.

a) fail, will kill

b) 'm going to grow, leave

c) 'm never going to read, 've taken

d) 'll like, get

e) isn't coming out, 's done

f) finish, 'm going to set up

6 Students work individually to complete the sentences. They then compare with a partner.

Backpacking (p 115)

Closed books. Brainstorm different types of holidays people can take (package holidays, skiing holidays, camping holidays, etc.). Find out if students have ever travelled alone or with friends. Where did they go? Did they have any exciting/frightening experiences? Encourage them to tell the rest of the class their stories.

Reading (p 115)

1 Groupwork. Students discuss the questions and report back to the class.

2 Students read the text. Ask them what they think *to take something with a pinch of salt* means (to regard something as unlikely to be true) and why they should view traveller's tales with scepticism.

Because travellers love to exaggerate and embellish their stories.

3 Whole class. Ask students to call out the words and expressions as they find them.

a) buzz

b) tales

c) exaggerate and embellish

d) dodging

e) part of the rite of passage from child to adult

4 Students read the two versions of Tom's story and say which they prefer and why.

Lexis (p 116)

1 Ask students the first question and then put them in pairs to find ten more examples of exaggerated language in version 2 of Tom's story. The should list this together with the less dramatic language from version 1 which it replaces.

dirty/filthy

full of / swarming with

big ants / huge ants

which had swollen up / which had swollen up like a balloon

trying to kill them / going berserk trying to kill them

I hit it / I bashed it

I fainted / I blacked out

had hit my head / had dented my skull

I was taken to hospital / I was rushed to hospital

I had five stitches / I had emergency surgery

2 Pairwork. Both versions of Tom's second story contain a mixture of normal and exaggerated language. The students should choose the most dramatic expression in each case to re-write the story. You may need to explain that a latrine is a toilet. Do not check answers at this stage.

3 🔲 **61 SB p 158**

Play the recording for students to listen and check their stories.

🔲 **61**
Tom's second story

While I was travelling, I got an incredibly painful tropical ear infection after I fell into a stinking latrine. Feeling like death, I lay in bed with a raging

*fever for what felt like a lifetime. Wracked with
pain, I couldn't face eating anything, and I lost so
much weight that I looked like a skeleton.
Eventually, I managed to get hold of some
antibiotics which brought me back from death's
door.*

4   Students match the expressions with their meanings.

> a 9   b 4   c 10   d 2   e 7   f 1   g 5   h 8   i 6
> j 3

5   Students choose five expressions and use them in
sentences. Allow them to compare with a partner and then
get some students to read their sentences to the class.

6   Pairwork. Students read the notes and prepare their stories.
Remind them that the Language toolbox contains useful
linking expressions to help them. Go round offering help
and advice where necessary.

> *Sample answer*
>
> People were packed like sardines into the boat,
> which was only a tiny fishing boat. Then, ten
> minutes into the journey, the sky turned dangerously
> black and a ferocious storm blew up. The sea, which
> had been peaceful and calm when we left the
> harbour, was suddenly heaving with mountainous
> waves, crashing down on us. Thinking that we were
> going to be tipped into the shark-infested water at
> any moment, to our horror we noticed there were
> no lifejackets or radio in the boat. We thought it
> was the end for all of us. Finally, after a brief period
> of screaming and crying, I blacked out with fear.

7   Pairs join other pairs to tell their stories. Go around and
listen for any particularly good ones that can be shared
with the class.

Job hunting (p 117)

Closed books. Find out what students think is the best way of
finding a job in their countries. Would they look in the
newspapers? Would they write letters to companies asking if
they have any vacancies? Would they use the Internet? What
things would they tell a prospective employer about
themselves?

CVs (p 117)

1   Explain that a CV or curriculum vitae is a document used
in many countries to tell a prospective employer about a
job applicant. As well as giving the name, address and
phone number of the applicant, it usually lists his or her
educational details and qualifications together with an
employment history. There may also be a section for
personal interests and the names of people who will act as
referees – saying that they know the applicant and believe
them to be honest, hard-working, etc.

Write DOs and DON'Ts on the board. Then go through the
list of tips for writing a CV with the class and ask them to
say which column they should go in. Note: the advice to
'embellish' your good points does not mean you should
tell lies, or exaggerate so much that your claims are
unbelievable. However, you should make them sound as
good as possible. Exercise 3 will provide some good ideas
of how this can be done.

> DO
> b)   sound enthusiastic
> d)   emphasise your good points and embellish
>   them where possible
> f)   keep it simple
> h)   check your typing, spelling and punctuation
> j)   include dates
>
> DON'T
> a)   mention your bad points or failures
> c)   be funny or too informal
> e)   sound desperate
> g)   use decorative devices or lots of different fonts
> i)   use family or friends as referees
> k)   include irrelevant information

2   Students read Ben's CV and say where he has gone wrong
according to the tips in 1.

> He has done almost everything you shouldn't do.
> a)   He mentions that he has failed his history
>   A-level.
> c)   'Did some babysitting' is too informal, and
>   inclusion of 'Donating blood' under Personal
>   interests is a failed attempt at humour. His
>   e-mail address is also unlikely to impress an
>   employer.
> g)   He has used a decorative border.
> h)   There are several typing errors.
> i)   He has used his mother as a referee.
> k)   The parts about babysitting and donating blood
>   are irrelevant.

3   Students match the items in list A with the embellishments
in list B.

> a 6   b 2   c 5   d 3   e 4   f 1

4   Students re-write Ben's CV. Encourage them to finish this
before looking at the improved version on page 140.

Character reference (p 118)

1 Students read Pete's reference and say what impression of Ben they get from it.

> A very positive impression.

2 📼 **62 SB p 158**

Play the recording. Students then say whether the reference or the conversation gives the most truthful impression of Ben's character.

> The conversation.

📼 **62**

(P = Pete; K = Kate)

P: *Come in!*

K: *Hi, Pete – I just wondered if you fancied coming out for a coffee.*

P: *Oh, I was just writing a letter.*

K: *Writing a letter! Is your phone out of order?*

P: *No – well, not exactly a letter. Ben's applied for a job at a children's summer camp, and they've asked me for a character reference. He must have put me down as one of his referees.*

K: *Oh dear – you're not going to tell them the truth, are you?*

P: *What do you mean?*

K: *Well, that he's a big-headed show-off who goes out every night and never does a day's work.*

P: *Oh, come on, he's not that bad – I mean, kids love him. He's always entertaining his little brother's friends with his magic tricks and silly jokes.*

K: *Oh yes, he's great with children – but he's a big kid himself, isn't he?*

P: *Yes, I suppose he is a bit immature.*

K: *And I hope they don't expect him to work before four o'clock in the afternoon. You know what he's like – he needs a bomb under him to get him up in the morning.*

P: *Mm.*

K: *Also, he hates taking orders from anybody. Do you remember that job he had last summer in a restaurant? He ended up throwing a bucket of water over the chef when she asked him to wash the kitchen floor.*

P: *Oh no, don't remind me. He won't do anything he doesn't enjoy, will he? Mind you, he did run that restaurant single-handed when the chef and two of the waiters were off sick with food poisoning.*

K: *That's true. He's good in a crisis. But having said that, he's good at causing a crisis as well – I mean, you know the food poisoning was his fault, don't you?*

P: *Oh, yes – oh dear, this isn't helping.*

K: *Hey, do you think he's still got blue hair?*

P: *Come on. Let's go and get that coffee.*

3 Pairwork. Students match the extracts from the conversation with the corresponding parts of the reference. Check answers with the class.

> a) ... he may not be best suited to early morning tasks.
>
> b) ... shows great initiative under pressure.
>
> c) While his critics may see him as a bit of a trouble-maker ...
>
> d) Ben's appearance is unconventional ...
>
> e) Ben is a natural leader ...
>
> f) ... he is very good at relating to them (children) on their own level.
>
> g) He is self-assured, outgoing and extremely sociable.

4 Whole class. Give students time to think of their answers to these questions. Then ask several students for their answers.

Angels (p 119)

Song

1 Ask students to name other songs by Robbie Williams.

> *Possible answers*
> Let Me Entertain You
> Old Before I Die
> Millennium
> Rock DJ
> Kids

2 Pairwork. Students read the lyrics and try to supply the missing words. Do not check answers at this stage.

3 📼 **63 SB p 158**

Play the recording for students to check their answers.

> 1 wait
> 2 know
> 3 old
> 4 bed
> 5 dead
> 6 protection
> 7 take
> 8 weak
> 9 above
> 10 grows
> 11 dead

63

Angels by Robbie Williams

I sit and wait.
Does an angel contemplate my fate?
And do they know,
The places where we go
When we're grey and old?
'Cos I have been told
That salvation lets their wings unfold.
So when I'm lying in my bed,
Thoughts running through my head,
And I feel that love is dead,
I'm loving angels instead.

And through it all
She offers me protection
A lot of love and affection,
Whether I'm right or wrong.
And down the waterfall,
Wherever it may take me,
I know that life won't break me,
When I come to call, she won't forsake me,
I'm loving angels instead.

When I'm feeling weak,
And my pain walks down a one way street,
I look above,
And I know I'll always be blessed with love.
And as the feeling grows,
She breathes flesh to my bones.
And when love is dead,
I'm loving angels instead.

4 Explain that someone's *frame of mind* is how they are feeling, or their mood. Go through the words in the box and ask students to say which ones they think best fit Robbie Williams' frame of mind when he wrote this song.

> thoughtful, reflective, spiritual, philosophical, grateful

Follow-up activity

There are quite a lot of words in *Angels* which have a religious flavour (*forsake, salvation, flesh, angels, blessed*). Discuss with your class whether they feel Robbie Williams is a religious person or if he's using the 'angels' as a metaphor for a religious/philosophical awakening of some sort in his life. (He had just gone through a difficult stage in his life after being fired from the boy band, *Take That*, and was starting his solo career.)

5 Pairwork. Students discuss their reactions to the song.

Test

Scoring: one point per correct answer unless otherwise indicated.

1
1 'm taking
2 'll be
3 'm going to travel
4 'll need
5 'm going to go
6 might do
7 'm going to buy
8 'll have saved
9 'll be getting
10 'll have travelled

2 (2 points per correct answer)
1 'm going to visit
2 starts
3 'll be
4 's written
5 'm starting / start
6 'll have finished
7 'll be sitting
8 'll meet
9 doesn't leave

3
1 heart
2 qualifications
3 grant
4 fail
5 attention
6 enrol

4
1 door
2 tears
3 blowing
4 moon
5 stiff
6 breath

12 *Student* Test

Name: _____   **Total:** _____ /40

---

1 Future forms 1 *10 points*
Underline the correct form.

I (1) **taking / 'm taking** my final exams this summer and then I (2) **would be / 'll be** free – no more school for me. When I finish the exams I (3) **'m going to travel / 'll go to travel** round the world for a year. Of course, I (4) **'ll need / 'm needing** to do some work while I'm travelling, so I (5) **would go / 'm going to go** to the Careers Advice office next week to find out about casual work in Australia and the United States. I (6) **might do / 'll have done** some work like fruit-picking or farming, if I can, because I like to be outdoors.

I (7) **buy / 'm going to buy** my ticket next month – I (8) **'ll save / 'll have saved** enough money by then. It's amazing to think that in only two months' time, I (9) **'m getting / 'll be getting** on a plane to New York and a year from now I (10) **'ll have travelled / 'll travel** half way round the world. I can't wait for it to start!

2 Future forms 2 *18 points*
Complete with an appropriate future form.

1   Josy is finally back from her travels, so I _____ (visit) her tomorrow.

2   The film _____ (start) at 8.30.

3   I think it _____ (be) worth a fortune in a few years' time.

4   He isn't leaving the office until he _____ (written) his report.

5   I _____ (start) Russian lessons next term.

6   By the end of next week I _____ (finish) all my exams.

7   By this time next week she _____ (sit) on a beach and drinking cocktails.

8   OK, I _____ (meet) you outside the theatre at six.

9   She's going to be late if she _____ (not leave) now.

3 Vocabulary – education *6 points*
Complete the sentences with a suitable word.

1   My father can still remember poems that he learnt by _____ when he was at school.

2   To get a top job you need work experience as well as good academic _____ .

3   I don't know if I can afford to go to university unless I get a _____ .

4   If you _____ an exam, you may be able to retake it the following year.

5   Tina didn't pay _____ in class, so she found the exams very difficult.

6   Next week I'm going to _____ for a place at the teacher training college.

4 Vocabulary – exaggerated language *6 points*
Complete the sentences with an appropriate word.

1   I was at death's _____ .

2   I burst into _____ .

3   It was mind-_____ .

4   I was over the _____ .

5   I was scared _____ .

6   It took my _____ away.

13 *Home* Overview

The topic of this unit is the different places people call *home*. The main grammar focus is on the passive.

Students start by discussing what *home* means to them and describing their homes and the objects in them. They listen to a psychologist talking about how people's characters are reflected in their surroundings and match people to rooms. They then talk about their favourite rooms.

Students talk about breakfast around the world and read an article about Feng Shui which places great importance on the arrangement of the room in which you start the day.

Students then read a text on a new ship which is being designed as a place for thousands of people to live. They discuss whether they would like to live there and then examine the use of the passive voice in the text.

The unit ends with a look at websites. Students look at the Rough Guides home page and match extracts to the web pages linked to it. They then discuss, plan and write a website for their class.

Section	Aims	What the students are doing
Introduction page 120	*Conversation skills*: fluency work	Discussing what *home* means to you.
Ideal homes pages 120–122	*Lexis*: words describing homes	Describing homes, parts of houses and the objects in them.
	Speaking skills: description	
	Listening skills: listening for gist	Listening to a psychologist and matching people to rooms.
	Conversation skills: fluency work	Anecdote: talking about your favourite room.
Close up pages 122–123	*Grammar*: quantity	Using quantity expressions to describe your environment.
Rise and shine pages 124–125	*Conversation skills*: fluency work	Discussing breakfast habits in the students' country and around the world.
	Reading skills: reading for detail	Reading an article on Feng Shui and its recommendations for the place where you eat breakfast.
		Answering a questionnaire on breakfast.
The Freedom Ship pages 126–127	*Reading skills*: skimming	Reading a text on an unusual new ship and answering questions.
Close up page 128	*Grammar*: the passive	Examining passive sentences from the reading text to establish form and usage of the passive.
		Using the passive to complete descriptions of famous structures.
Home page pages 129–130	*Reading skills*: reading for gist	Looking at the Rough Guides home page and matching texts to web pages.
	Conversation skills: fluency work	Discussing, designing and writing material for a class home page.
	Writing skills: home pages	

13 Home Teacher's notes

Closed books. Write on the board *Home is where the heart is*. Ask students what they think this saying means and whether or not they agree with it.

Whole class. Ask students what home means to them and elicit four or five responses before going through the nine quotations in the book. Then ask which of these the students most relate to.

Ideal homes (p 120)

Lexis

1 Students work individually to complete the sentences and then compare their answers with a partner.

2 Pairwork. Students take turns to describe three houses (or flats) they like. Remind them that they can find some useful language for talking about homes in the Language toolbox.

3 Students match the objects with the house parts individually and then compare with a partner.

> *Possible answers*
> a) 6 (perhaps also 1 and 4)
> b) 5 (also 7 and perhaps 4)
> c) 1
> d) 7 (perhaps also 4 and 5)
> e) 3
> f) 2
> g) 4

4 Pairwork. Students tell each other which of these things they have and in which part of the house.

5 Pairwork. Establish that *to have something in common* means to share features or characteristics. Students discuss what all the items in each group have in common.

> A   Things you find on the floor.
> B   Things you find on windows.
> C   Things you find on walls.
> D   Things you find on or near the front door.

6 Students complete the sentences making them true for themselves. Ask several students to read their sentences to the class.

Listening (p 121)

1 Pairwork. Students look at the pictures and discuss the questions. They then report back to the class.

2 Whole class. Go through the instructions with the class. Then read each statement and ask students to say which room it goes with. See how much agreement there is in the class.

3 🔲 **64 SB p 158**
Play the recording for students to listen to and check their answers.

> a) Room 1   b) Room 1   c) Room 2   d) Room 2
> e) Room 1   f) Room 2

🔲 **64**
Room 1
At first sight this room looks a bit of a mess. A real eccentric lives here. You can tell it's a woman because there are piles of cushions everywhere – men don't like cushions. Cushions may look attractive, but nine times out of ten, they don't make seats more comfortable. But that's typical of the different ways men and women approach homes – men tend to be more practical, whilst women are more concerned with aesthetics.

The room is extremely cluttered – there's far too much stuff, and every surface is covered. There isn't really enough furniture here – she could do with a few shelves or cupboards to put all this stuff in. But this is not a practical person. This is somebody who lives in the world of imagination – perhaps a children's book writer.

There's nothing calming about this room – there are loads of bright colours, but no pastels at all. Also, there's very little natural light and not many indoor plants. More green would help bring this person down to earth. But the bright colours definitely suggest a person who is warm-hearted and sociable. In fact, judging by the number of candles and full ashtrays, I'd say she's a bit of a party animal.

Room 2
This one's more difficult because there are very few clues here about the type of person who lives in it. I think it's a man because there are hardly any personal objects on display – for instance, there aren't any family photos around the place.

But there's plenty of evidence to suggest that he's a successful career man, someone who spends most of his time travelling. There are a couple of oriental rugs which are probably worth a lot of money, and a few other ornaments which suggest that he travels to the Far East.

Most of the furniture is functional rather than decorative. I think this is somebody who doesn't actually spend much time at home, and when he does, he's obsessively tidy. The lack of decoration suggests that he wants to be ready to pack his bags and leave at short notice.

He has little time to socialise, except in a working context, and probably never entertains at home. He's single, and may be the sort of person who has problems with commitment in personal relationships.

4 Whole class. Find out if students agree with what the psychologist says. They can then turn to page 138 to read what the people themselves say.

Anecdote (p 122)

(See the Introduction on page 4 for more ideas on how to set up, monitor and repeat 'anecdotes'.)

Pairwork. Give students time to read the questions and think about what they are going to say. They then take turns to describe their favourite rooms.

Close up (p 122)

Quantity

1 Pairwork. Students look at the two groups of extracts and decide what those in each group have in common. It might help to tell them to ignore the underlined expressions at this stage.

> All the extracts in group A contain countable nouns.
> All the extracts in group B contain uncountable nouns.

2 Students replace the underlined quantity expressions in 1 with alternatives from the list. Check answers with the class before going on to the next exercise. If they have difficulty with quantity expressions, go through the Language reference section on page 123 with them.

> a 5   b 2   c 7   d 8   e 6   f 1   g 4   h 3

3 Students work individually to complete the sentences so that they are true for themselves. They then compare with a partner.

4 Whole class. Ask several students to read the sentences aloud. Then elicit answers to the questions.

> a) a little English, a few things
> b) a little, a few
> c) little
> d) few

5 Students complete the sentences with appropriate expressions from the box. Check answers with the class.

> a) a little
> b) a few
> c) Few
> d) a little
> e) few
> f) little

6 Whole class. Go through the statements one by one, asking individual students to choose the correct verb form. Students then work individually to change the statements so that they describe their home town and to write two more statements. They then compare answers with a partner.

> a) isn't
> b) 's
> c) are
> d) 's
> e) are
> f) 's

Rise and shine (p 124)

Closed books. Write the words *owls* and *larks* on the board. Explain that owls are people who function best at night. They can stay up late without feeling tired, but may find it difficult to get up in the morning. They can be bad-tempered if you try to have a conversation with them too early in the morning.

Larks are people who get tired in the evening and find it very difficult to stay up late. They rarely stay long at parties. However, they find it easy to get up early in the morning and that is when they are most cheerful and do their best work.

Students discuss whether they are owls or larks. Find out how many fit in each category.

1 Whole class. This could be a mingling exercise with students moving around the classroom trying to find a name to put against each question. You could also organise it as a race, with the first person to put a name to each question being the winner.

2 Pairwork. Students look at the food and drink items in the box and answer the questions. If anyone asks you which country the items come from, do not answer at this stage.

3 🔲 **65 SB p 159**
Before you play the recording, ask students to say which country's typical breakfast each item comes from. Some items can go with more than one country. Then play the recording for them to check their answers.

> USA: eggs sunny side up, bacon, pancakes, toast, orange juice, coffee

Germany: jam, cereal, cold meat, cheese, bread rolls, coffee (or tea), boiled eggs (with salt and pepper)

Japan: green tea, rice, miso soup, pickled vegetables, grilled fish, omelette

▭ 65

Lizanne

(I = Interviewer; L = Lizanne)

I: *Lizanne, you're from America. What do you have for breakfast?*

L: *Er, eggs, bacon, pancakes, and a bit of toast on the side.*

I: *And what to drink?*

L: *Usually we start with orange juice and have lots and lots of coffee.*

I: *And your eggs – how do you like to have them done?*

L: *Sunny side up.*

I: *What does that mean?*

L: *That means that the yolk is facing upward – it's not been turned over.*

I: *Thank you.*

Nicola

(I = Interviewer; N = Nicola)

I: *Nicola, you're from Germany. Tell me about breakfast. What do you have for breakfast?*

N: *Well, in Germany it's different. Some people like jam or cereals, but the typical breakfast is, of course, with cold meat like salami, bacon or ham, and cheese. And we always have hot bread rolls and coffee. But I don't like coffee very much. And, of course, boiled eggs – they are very important in Germany and very typical, with salt or pepper.*

I: *You don't drink coffee for breakfast. What do you like?*

N: *I like to drink tea.*

Michiko

(I = Interviewer; M = Michiko)

I: *Michiko. What do you have for breakfast? What do you have to drink for breakfast?*

M: *We drink green tea for breakfast.*

I: *OK, and what about, what do you eat?*

M: *We eat rice, miso soup, pickled vegetables, er, grilled fish – like salmon, and Japanese omelette, and seaweed.*

I: *What, what do you have in the Japanese omelette? What does that ...*

M: *Japanese omelette is sweet taste, and it's different from the western omelette.*

I: *And miso soup. What is in that?*

M: *Miso soup is a salty soup, which often has seaweed, vegetables and tofu.*

4   Pairwork. Students take turns to describe the most unusual breakfast they've ever had. Encourage them to report any interesting information back to the class.

Reading (p 124)

1   Whole class. Focus attention on the picture and elicit suggestions as to why this kitchen might not be a good place to start your day. Don't confirm or reject any ideas they have.

2   Go through the information about Feng Shui in the margin. Then ask students to read the text and find eight ways to improve the room in the picture according to the principles of Feng Shui.

1	The kitchen should be clutter-free. (No washing-up from last night on the work surface.)
2	Use bright colours, like red and yellow.
3	Decorate with pastel greens and blues.
4	Choose pastel greens and blues for the plates and bowls.
5	Use wooden worktops and tables, and ceramic tiles for the floors.
6	The breakfast place should be facing east.
7	Create a Feng Shui environment with plants and fresh flowers.
8	Have a picture of something that motivates.

3   Whole class. Read each sentence in turn and ask students to scan the text for words and expressions to replace the underlined ones.

a)	bleary-eyed
b)	get off on the wrong foot; goes from bad to worse
c)	clutter-free
d)	rising; holiday destination

4   Pairwork. Students take turns asking questions to find out if the statements in 3 are true for their partners.

5   Pairwork. Students answer the questionnaire. Make sure they answer all the questions before they turn to page 137 to check their answers.

The Freedom Ship (p 126)

Closed books. Ask students to tell you about the most unusual home they know, have heard of or can imagine.

Reading (p 126)

1 Whole class. Students look at the illustration and discuss the advantages and disadvantages of living on a ship like this.

2 Pairwork. Encourage students to fill in numbers without looking ahead to the article. Reassure them that there are no penalties for getting it wrong; you just want them to discuss in pairs and decide what they think the most likely numbers are. When they have finished, they can read the article and see how close they were.

> 1 1.3 kilometres
> 2 thirty storeys
> 3 65,000
> 4 25
> 5 two
> 6 150,000
> 7 4.2 million
> 8 5.4 billion

3 Students read the article again and find answers to the questions.

> a) Two years.
> b) In Florida / At sea.
> c) To ensure a crime-free environment.
> d) To design the best place in the world for living and having fun.
> e) Its immense size.
> f) The airport on the ship's top deck.
> g) Dr John Brown and other ship engineers.
> h) Buyers of the first two thousand apartments are being offered a 35% discount.

4 Whole class. Go through the statements one by one and ask students to scan the text for words and expressions to replace the underlined ones.

> a) circumnavigate the globe
> b) vessel
> c) screened
> d) inspiration for
> e) withstand
> f) *pièce de résistance*
> g) scepticism
> h) arouse

5 Whole class. Read the instructions and start a discussion about how possible or desirable the project is. Ask students to say whether they would like to live on the ship and why or why not.

Close up (p 128)

The passive

1 Students match the beginnings and endings of the sentences. Encourage them to do this without looking back at the article. When they have finished, they can look back and check their answers.

> a 2   b 5   c 4   d 3   e 6   f 1

2 Pairwork. Students discuss the questions. Check answers with the class. If students have difficulty with the passive, refer them to the Language reference section.

> a) be
> b) Past: b5, e6, f1. Present: d3. Future: a2, c4.
> c) b5
> d) by

3 Students use appropriate passive forms to complete the texts. They then decide which two famous structures are being described. They can check their answers on page 136.

> A (The Berlin Wall)
> 1 had been divided
> 2 were separated
> 3 was finally dismantled
> 4 had been erected
>
> B (La Sagrada Familia, Barcelona)
> 1 was laid
> 2 is still being built
> 3 has recently been speeded up
> 4 will never be finished
> 5 should be left

4 Pairwork. Students look at questions 1–3 and answer questions a–c.

> a) What has recently speeded up the work?
> b) We have no information about precisely who performed the actions.
> c) You use the passive when you don't know who performed the action.

5 Go through the examples with the class. Students then work individually to make their lists of changes. They then compare lists with a partner and discuss whether the changes have been positive or negative.

Home page (p 129)

Reading

1 Give students plenty of time to study the Rough Guides home page and to discuss it in pairs or small groups. Make sure that everyone understands that a home page is like the contents page of a book. It tells you what you can find on a website and you click on different sections within it to move to further web pages on the same website. You could ask students who are familiar with the Internet to explain this to the others. They then match the extracts to the numbered sections of the home page.

Note: Rough Guides started out as a company publishing travel guides. They have now expanded to offer guides to other things as music and even the Internet itself.

> a) 6   b) 3   c) 2   d) 5   e) 1   f) 4

Optional activity

If you have classroom access to the Internet, go to the Rough Guides home page and allow students to look at some of the material that is there.

2 Groupwork. Students look at the class home page. They discuss the sort of information that might be on the linked web pages. They then report back to the class.

3 In the same groups, students think about their own design for a home page and suggest ideas for different hypertext links. Again, they report back to the class. Find out what the class think most Internet surfers would be most interested in finding out about them.

4 Groupwork. Groups decide which web page(s) each is going to be responsible for. They then write text to go on the web pages they have chosen. Display the work on the classroom wall for everyone to read and enjoy. Of course, if you actually can set up a website, you could get the students to put their work on the Internet for other people to access.

Test

Scoring: one point per correct answer unless otherwise indicated.

1 (2 points per correct answer)
1   are being built
2   was sent
3   have been lost
4   will be opened
5   is being repaired
6   was taken

2 (2 points per correct answer)
1   was built
2   has been very well maintained
3   has been recently redecorated
4   was used
5   has been completely modernised
6   were fitted
7   is included / will be included
8   was being used / was used

3 1   Several of
2   too much
3   hardly any
4   loads of
5   many
6   Most of my
7   a little
8   None of

4 1   shelves
2   radiators
3   power points
4   doorbell

Home Test

Name: **Total:** _____ /40

1 The passive (1) *12 points*

Complete the sentences with the correct form of the passive.

1 They're building two new houses.

   Two new houses _____ .

2 The judge sent the man to prison.

   The man _____ to prison.

3 We have lost your medical records.

   Your medical records _____ .

4 They'll open the new supermarket tomorrow.

   The new supermarket _____
   tomorrow.

5 The garage in town is repairing my car.

   My car _____ by the
   garage in town.

6 Julie's mother took her to the dentist.

   Julie _____ to the dentist
   by her mother.

2 The passive (2) *16 points*

Put the verbs into the appropriate passive form.

Do go in, Mr and Mrs Johnson, and have a good look

around. This house (1) _____ (build)

in the 1930s. It (2) _____ (very well

maintain), as you can see. In fact, most of the house

(3) _____ (recently redecorate). This

room in front of you (4) _____ (use)

as a study by the previous owners. The bathroom, as you

can see, (5) _____ (completely

modernise). The bedrooms (6) _____

(fit) with double glazing a year ago. Now, you know that

all the furniture in the house (7) _____

(include) in the sale, as the owners have moved abroad.

Now if you'd like to follow me outside … Oh, did I

mention the garage (8) _____ (use)

as a workshop until recently, so it needs a bit of a clean-up,

to be honest. The garden is beautiful, though …

3 Quantifiers *8 points*

Underline the correct alternative.

1 **Several / Several of** these buildings date back to the
   sixteenth century.

2 Footballers earn far **too much / too many** money.

3 I've bought **hardly any / none** new clothes this year.

4 Jane has got **loads of / several of** friends.

5 Dave doesn't know **few / many** of his neighbours.

6 **Most of my / Most of** time is spent cleaning up after
   you!

7 I'm quite full, actually. I'll just have **a little / a few**
   cake.

8 **None of / None** my family likes pasta.

4 Vocabulary – houses *4 points*

Complete the missing words in these sentences.

1 I must put up some s_____ for my books.

2 The house is so warm since we got those new

   r_____ fitted.

3 We need some new p_____ p_____
   in this room. There's nowhere to plug in the stereo.

4 I rang the d_____ , but I don't think it works,
   so I knocked on the door until she heard me.

14 *Review 2* *Teacher's notes*

Don't quote me on that! (p 131)

Reporting verbs

a) suggested to journalists
b) advised his colleagues
c) explained to the press
d) told a conference
e) admitted to the questioner
f) announced to the American people

a 4   b 5   c 3   d 1   e 6   f 2

Dilemma (p 131)

Unreal conditionals

1   a 3   b 2   c 6   d 1   e 5   f 4

2   Groupwork. Students discuss the questions in 1.

3   Students work individually to write their questions, then mingle and ask their classmates. The class then decide who gave the most interesting or unusual answers.

Unsolved mysteries (p 132)

Modals of deduction

1   Groupwork. Students work in threes and each member of the group reads a different extract. They then tell their stories to the others. Encourage them to do this without reading the original extract.

2   Groupwork. Students use the words in the box to discuss the mysteries.

School daze (p 133)

Narrative tense structures

1   a)
1   was sitting
2   asked
3   had been
4   were brought
5   enjoyed
6   was

7   had failed ('d failed)
8   had performed
9   hadn't been wearing

b)
10   was sitting
11   continued
12   had told
13   tried
14   told
15   had already failed
16   asked
17   replied
18   had never seen
19   pushed
20   ran

2   66 SB p 159

Play the recording for students to listen to and check their answers.

 66

a)

A student at Oxford was sitting an exam when he asked a supervisor for a glass of red wine and a plate of scones, correctly adding that this tradition had been the right of Oxford scholars dating back to medieval times. The wine and the scones were brought to the exam room, and the student enjoyed the lot before finishing his exam. A few weeks later, the student was shocked to find that he'd failed the exam, not because he had performed badly, but because he hadn't been wearing his sword as he sat the exam.

b)

A student who was sitting an exam continued to write a full five minutes after the professor had told everyone to stop. When the student tried to hand in his paper, the professor told him not to bother, as he had already failed. 'Do you know who I am?' the student angrily asked the professor. When the professor replied that he had never seen the student before, the student pushed his paper into the middle of the pile of other papers and quickly ran out of the room.

3   Whole class. Students discuss the question.

The *Harry Potter* phenomenon
(p 133)

Relative clauses (non-defining & defining)

> a) whose
> b) which / that / –
> c) who
> d) who
> e) which
> f) which

The thing I ... (p 133)

Emphasis (cleft sentences)

1
> a) The thing I like most (*or* most *like*) about ... is ...
> b) One of the things I don't like about ... is ...
> c) What I don't understand about ... is ...
> d) What really annoys me about ... is ...
> e) The thing I find really amusing about ... is ...
> f) One thing I've always hated about ... is ...

2 Groupwork. Students show their completed sentences to each other and discuss them.

3 Students make further sentences about another topic from the box in 1.

Revved up or relaxed? (p 134)

Future forms

1
> 1 will be doing
> 2 are going
> 3 are going to be
> 4 will have made
> 5 are you doing
> 6 will you have decided, are going to do
> 7 will you buy
> 8 are going to do

2 Students answer the questionnaire and exchange it with a partner. They then read the analysis to see what the scores mean.

I've got loads of ... (p 135)

Quantity

Go through the rules with the class. Students then play the game in groups.

Language trivia quiz (p 135)

Passive structures

1
> a) is thought, is spoken, is currently learnt
> b) is used
> c) is suggested, will be held
> d) are spoken
> e) is expressed
> f) is reckoned
> g) is estimated, was invented

2 Students try to guess the correct answer for each of the sentences in 1. They then check their answers.

End Of Course Test

> Scoring: one point per correct answer unless otherwise indicated.
>
> **1**
> 1 admitted
> 2 refused
> 3 invited
> 4 reassured
> 5 insisted
> 6 complained
> 7 advised
> 8 told
> 9 claimed
> 10 explained
>
> **2** (2 points per correct answer)
> 1 did you have your hair done
> 2 had it cut
> 3 haven't had my car repaired
> 4 we're having all our valuables photographed
> 5 to have any photocopying done
>
> **3** (2 points per correct answer)
> 1 won, would, spend
> 2 were, would, have
> 3 had, would, wish
>
> **4**
> 1 must
> 2 can't
> 3 must
> 4 can't
> 5 can't

6 can't
7 must
8 must
9 can't
10 can't

5 (2 points per correct answer)
1 had spent
2 spotted
3 was watching
4 shouted
5 had been raised
6 announced
7 included
8 saw
9 was waving
10 was read
11 contacted
12 organised
13 had been living
14 never made
15 can
16 've found

6 1 which
2 whose
3 who
4 whose
5 which
6 which
7 who
8 who
9 whose
10 who

7 1 hate, about
2 don't, understand
3 really, annoys
4 thing, found

8 (2 points per correct answer)
1 's going
2 'm going to try
3 'll be
4 leaves
5 'll pay
6 'll be lying
7 'll be doing
8 'll have been married
9 's starting

9 1 few
2 loads of
3 any
4 enough
5 none
6 a lot of
7 Most
8 few
9 plenty

10 (2 points per correct answer)
1 The post is delivered every morning.
2 It'll have to be done soon.
3 He's already been offered the job.
4 A 35% discount is being offered.
5 The stolen goods were found yesterday.
6 The suspects were being followed.

11 1 breath
2 -detached
3 foot
4 long-winded
5 complete
6 contracted
7 loft
8 -conscious
9 scientific
10 nose
11 level-headed
12 Brand
13 -seeing
14 skin
15 heart-throb
16 bored
17 confined
18 genetic
19 extremely
20 sensitive
21 enrol
22 heart
23 -rise
24 nipped
25 absent-minded

14 End Of Course Test

Name: _____   Total: _____ /150

1 Reporting verbs *10 points*

Underline the correct words.

1 They **admitted / told** that they'd been speeding.

2 She **denied / refused** to say what had happened.

3 Joe **insisted / invited** us to have dinner with them.

4 The representative **explained / reassured** them that nothing was wrong.

5 Shaun **insisted / persuaded** on telling the truth.

6 The customer **complained / argued** to the manager.

7 We **advised / suggested** them to contact their solicitors.

8 He **announced / told** us that he had resigned.

9 She **claimed / reassured** to her that she had been at home all evening.

10 He **informed / explained** to her that he had to go away for a while.

2 *Have something done* *10 points*

Complete the sentences with the appropriate form of the verbs.

A: When (1) _____ (your hair / do)?

B: I (2) _____ (it / cut) last week.

＊   ＊   ＊

A: Are we driving to the restaurant?

B: No, sorry. I (3) _____

_____ (my car / not repair) yet.

Let's call for a taxi.

＊   ＊   ＊

A: Why is that man taking photographs of all your things?

B: Oh, we (4) _____

_____ (all our valuables / photograph) in case we get burgled.

A: But you haven't got any valuables!

＊   ＊   ＊

A: Where can I photocopy these files?

B: You should ask the office secretary if you need

(5) _____
(any photocopying / do).

3 Unreal conditionals *6 points*

Complete the gaps with suitable verbs.

1 Imagine you _____ £1 million in the lottery, how _____ you _____ the money?

2 Suppose you _____ disfigured in a car accident, _____ you _____ cosmetic surgery?

3 Assuming you _____ three wishes, what _____ you _____ for?

4 Modals of deduction *10 points*

Complete the sentences with *can't* or *must*.

1 Tammy and Michael have split up. He _____ have found out about all her affairs.

2 You _____ have seen Tom in the library today. He's in New York this week.

3 I'm sorry you didn't get my postcard. It _____ have got lost in the post.

4 That _____ be Bill's car. It's far too clean.

5 What a dreadful meeting. We _____ have agreed on more than three issues.

6 Tom is really pale after his holiday in Ibiza. He _____ have gone out in the sun at all.

7 I _____ have left my wallet in the car. Do you mind paying?

8 John _____ have gone out. I haven't seen him for hours.

9 It _____ be easy for you two, living so far apart from each other.

10 Jane _____ have stayed more than half an hour before she decided to go home.

5 Narrative tense structures *32 points*

Complete the article with the appropriate form of the verbs.

Luke Todds (1) _____ (spend) twenty-two years looking for this father before he (2) _____ (spot) him on the TV show, *Who wants to be a millionaire?* Luke (3) _____ (watch) the hit quiz show when he (4) _____ (shout), 'That's him!' Luke's hopes (5) _____ (raise) at the end of the previous show when the quiz master (6) _____ (announce) the list of contestants for the next show. They (7) _____ (include) 'Mark Todds'. And the next day he (8)_____ (see) his father. He (9) _____ (wave) at the cameras as his name (10) _____ (read) out. Luke's wife, Vicki, (11) _____ (contact) the show and (12) _____ (organise) a surprise reunion. Amazingly, father and son (13) _____ (live) just ten kilometres apart. Mark, sixty-four, who (14) _____ (never make) it onto the show's 'hot seat' said, 'They (15) _____ (can) keep the million pounds now that I (16) _____ (find) my son again.'

6 Relative clauses (non-defining & defining)
10 points

Complete the sentences with *which*, *who* or *whose*.

1   Guinness, _____ is a type of stout, originates from Ireland.

2   That's the boy _____ mother you had an argument with last week.

3   He's going out with a girl called Kim, _____ I don't get on with very well.

4   My brother, _____ obsession is surfing the Internet, is such a nerd.

5   She offered me a cigarette, _____ was strange. I thought she'd given up.

6   He's got a job _____ he loves.

7   Derek's got a younger brother _____ is married to my older sister.

8   I've got a friend _____ never turns up for anything on time.

9   Do you know Kerry, _____ mother works in that cabaret club?

10   My grandmother, _____ lived to ninety-one, was a great follower of politics.

7 Cleft sentences *8 points*

Complete the sentences with appropriate words.

1   What I h_____ a_____ this city is all the rubbish.

2   What I d_____ u_____ is why you never called me back.

3   What r_____ a_____ me in some restaurants is arrogant waiters!

4   The t_____ I f_____ most amusing in that film was the scene with the inflatable dinghy.

8 Future forms *18 points*

Put the verbs into an appropriate future form.

1   Do you know where he _____ (go) this evening?

2   When I leave school I _____ (try) to get a job in New York.

3   It _____ (be) a miracle if she's passed.

4   My flight _____ (leave) in one hour.

5   I _____ (pay) you now if you like.

6   This time next week I _____ (lie) on a beach.

7   Do you have any idea what you _____ (do) one year from now?

8   Next week we _____ (be married) for three years.

9   He _____ (start) his new course next week.

9 Quantity *9 points*

Underline the correct words.

1   There are very **few / little** opportunities in the film industry these days.

2   There are **much / loads of** mistakes in this.

3   There is hardly **any / some** wine left.

4   There isn't **plenty / enough** room for everybody.

5   There is **no / none** left.

6   There is **many / a lot of** pollution in this town.

7   **Most / Much** of my friends are single.

8   A **few / little** of these exercises are easy.

9   There is **hardly / plenty** of space.

10 Passive structures *12 points*

Rewrite the sentences in the passive

1 They deliver the post every morning.

   _____

   _____

2 You'll have to do it soon.

   _____

   _____

3 They've already offered him the job.

   _____

   _____

4 They're offering a 35% discount.

   _____

   _____

5 They found the stolen goods yesterday.

   _____

   _____

6 They were following the suspects.

   _____

   _____

11 Lexis *25 points*

Underline the correct words.

1 It was amazing. It took my **breath / mind** away.

2 I live in a semi-**terraced / -detached** house.

3 When he suggested going there, I had to put my **foot / hand** down.

4 Her speech was boring and **well-informed / long-winded**.

5 That was a **complete / thoroughly** waste of time!

6 Whilst living in Tanzania, Simon **contracted / tolerated** a tropical disease.

7 Go upstairs for me and get my suitcases from the **loft / cellar**.

8 Tim is really image-**conscious / -conscience**.

9 There have been a number of **scientist / scientific** breakthroughs in the field of cancer research.

10 Suzy's got a cute turned-up **nose / smile**.

11 I think I'm quite a **pretentious / level-headed** sort of person. I haven't done anything crazy yet!

12 **Brand / Client** loyalty means that you always buy the same make of product.

13 Did you enjoy the sight-**watching / -seeing** tour?

14 She's got perfect **skin / jaw**.

15 Oh, he's really gorgeous – what a **heart attack / heart-throb**!

16 I was **bored / afraid** stiff during that film.

17 Last year he spent three weeks **confined / restricted** to a wheelchair.

18 I'm really interested in the advances of **genetic / gene** engineering.

19 I'm always **totally / extremely** nervous before exams.

20 Jack's really **sensitive / laid-back**. He gets upset at the slightest thing.

21 He's going to **enrol / grant** for college this week.

22 I'm useless at learning things by **head / heart**.

23 He lives on the 6th floor of a high-**rise / -storey** building.

24 The dog got over-excited and **nipped / napped** the little girl on the leg.

25 Another word for *forgetful* is **stuck-up / absent-minded**.